STEEN EVALD
MEMORY OF LIGHT

ACC ART BOOKS

ON MEMORY OF LIGHT

Lars Schwander

> *The fact that experiences influence subsequent behaviour is evidence of an obvious but nevertheless remarkable activity called remembering. Memory is both a result of and an influence on perception, attention, and learning. The basic pattern of remembering consists of attention to an event followed by the representation of that event in the brain. Repeated attention, or practice, results in a cumulative effect on memory and enables activities such as a skillful performance on a musical instrument, the recitation of a poem, and reading and understanding words on a page.*
>
> (*Encyclopaedia Britannica* on Memory)

With his series "Memory of Light", photographer Steen Evald uncovers sculptural shapes. Seeking out the reflections of movement found in the moments where light meets body and shadow, "Memory of Light" is a playful inquiry into reflection, and one that leaves stark imprints, purified in penetrating white light. The images appear imaginative: they are extrovert and sculptural. But underneath their expressive appearance lives a puritan and humble principle: simplicity. A watchword for every step of the process. Nudity. Not to sexualize the physical related to the boudoir's fetishistic nature, but nudity because the photographer has needed to peel off as many layers as possible. Nudity because it removes the images from the historical quality of clothing – away from fashion, away from the tangible. The images' motif need not be anchored in time, but rather appears as abstraction.

The bodies, simply as sober figures in a closed space. Only this: the women, the light and the darkness. No disturbing elements, no superfluous effects, no real stage. Nudity belongs to no particular time or era; it is eternal, everlasting. Art and beauty are integrated elements. The school of art, its rules and aesthetics, is indeed the science of beauty. And beauty and the harmonic have always sought inspiration in the body's complete or partial nudity. In his project, Evald has described it as an exploration of the nude female form where a subtle movement conspires with the light. This, no matter whether it is deliberate or accidental – it always has decisive influence on the final image. "To me," he says, "these images are a step away from realism into a more abstract and ambiguous visual universe. Without focus, overexposed and with their blurred movements, it is like the women come from another place. Another dimension."

"Memory of Light" plays with photography itself. But not indifferently. Behind the spontaneous and frivolous abandon lies a deep and deliberate seriousness and – not least – concentration. As if he has reset, to start again from an absolute zero of photography. Sure, Evald has left some room for chance in movement itself, but the process is controlled in his determination of what he wants from each session. The resulting images – or shapes – are the amalgams of both his and the models' work. Evald has created a frame that allows complexity to arise from this interplay. Despite their movements' fleeting fluidity, these are not anonymous models. They are women of flesh and blood, with a name, with a specific presence. They are there, as luminous figures in the room. The images are created; as a memory for the photographer, a recollection rather than a documentation of this vision of light. Evald's photographic filtration of reality is complete.

While the movements in reality are three-dimensional, performed in colour and in a room with two interacting characters, the photograph compresses and distils this reality into a new and different existence. Suddenly the medium is two-dimensional, black and white, and the human characters have become mere figures. In this new reality, light shapes the language. It is the whiteness, this chalked light, that appears as the final matter of Evald's work, his alchemistic process. Usually, art is an expression of an imitation of reality.

Mimesis, basic theoretical principle in the creation of art. The word is Greek and means "imitation" (though in the sense of "re-presentation" rather than of "copying"). Plato and Aristotle spoke of mimesis as the re-presentation of nature. According to Plato, all artistic creation is a form of imitation: that which really exists (in the "world of ideas") is a type created by God; the concrete things man perceives in his existence are shadowy representations of this ideal type. Therefore, the painter, the tragedian, and the musician are imitators of an imitation, twice removed from the truth.

(*Encyclopaedia Britannica* on Mimesis)

These bodies of light have become figures of their own, emerging from the dark. In the movement they lift off, the bodies, like floating sculptures. Sometimes edgy and angular, sometimes almost fondling in their softness. I have seen angels in these images. I have seen torsos of marble, and I have seen things caught the moment before they disappear. Yes: ghostlike, misty, on their way back into the dark. Evald's photographs are like optical illusions. Photographs you can keep looking at to see a different image. And of course far from the symbiosis of Mimesis and Eros, where nude studies have become an art form of dauntlessness. No, that is not Evald's field at all. The core of these images, the prosaic narrative, is pure. As in: "undefiled". Equal, and sonorous – not far from music's need for harmony (and disharmony). It is a pursuit of the harmonic all while breaking with this self-same wish and ambition. As the American writer Julie Ralph expresses it:

Evald immerses us in a beautiful, dark abyss. Out of which emerge glimpses of the female form – a mysterious geometry of alluring lines and curves. Revealing portraits of naked women with a natural beauty that's baffling, beckoning and suddenly, in a split second, able to take our breath away. Evald opens an aperture into his soul. Seeking timeless beauty that's at once intimate and unapologetic. Striking. Enthralling. And stripped of superficialities. A universe where being naked almost becomes incidental.

(Julie Ralph, *Underneath it All*)

“Memory of Light” curiously blends Evald’s endeavour to work in the intersection between perfectionism and chance; the unforeseen. Because while you can control light and exposure, all the mechanics, to a certain point, without the element of chance, the asymmetrical, fundamentally arbitrary nature of movement, there will be no renewal. No creativity. In his own words: “They are graphic shapes, without an exacting definition.”

It cannot be emphasised enough how important it is to him to retain his first impression of each shoot as it happened. No changing of the characters. No manipulation of the photographs. Because it is the exact meeting between photographer and model that determined and still carries the final photograph’s meaning. What he saw, we see. The spectator sees. In a way, we become witnesses of Evald’s early ideas, like sketches in a notebook. Witnessing the point in the process where he made his decision. To compare this to chance performances is perhaps a stretch, as a shoot allows for many shots and movements and lighting changes. But with the wish to not manipulate his photographs in post-production, an authenticity is born. It is that feeling of abstraction and joy that shines through the surface.

Even if the images in many ways are carefully worked through both pre and post shooting, the project retains spontaneity, an almost playful lightness. The photographs are concurrently imaginary and staged, liberated from irrelevant – or immaterial – details. A reversed “tableau vivant” where live movement is frozen into stillness. As Evald puts it: “Born out of this elusive moment where magic happens – almost by accident. The women appear just as they are.” And, as such, an expression of the photographer’s inner dialogue, a sort of inner voice, in the moment of shooting. Like the symbiosis of the erotic, the imitation, or the portrayed and poetry.

> *Eros, Mimesis, Poiesis investigated the three key notions in Plato’s philosophical texts through dance practices. It established that dance was included in the Platonic Academy’s curriculum, as well as in the education of the guardians because, according to Plato, it is through dance that one learns to recognize measure, numbers, and*

what is rational. In The Republic, *Plato's dialogue on Justice and a privileged text of the liberal arts, he discusses the importance of an education in dance for a just and well ordered social and political life.*

(Mahnaz Yousefzadeh, *In the Beginning was Dance*)

Like the symbiosis of Eros, Mimesis and Poiesis, these nude studies work. As an art form of abstraction, Evald throws off the taboo in his depiction of real bodies, real skin, hair and gazes. The dissolution of the realistic reproduction reveals something dreamy, or even poetic. And, as such, the photographer refrains from speculation. From the outset, the wish has been to peel off all the layers. To enable up only with the very essence. An extract of his raw material, where he, the camera, the model and, not least, the light, filtrate this reality. No matter how beautiful these women are, and in spite of how real they are with their shapes, skin and hair, Evald has created a poetic parallel universe. A reflective image from which light radiates. Photographic images in their own right. Images that due to the abstraction, the process itself, have become universal. An abstraction prize.

Because the bodies are (obviously) fundamentally contorted. Twisted, or torn away from their natural shapes. The light and movements – not least – have created new facets of the models' original looks. There are even abstractions that the naked eye can't see. The whiteness seems to have a life of its own, there, among the shadows, stretched by the slow speed of exposure. That is how it came to be, that is how it appears, and that is how it remains. A journey into unknown land. And it has without a doubt been a journey for Evald to arrive at this: to create his own memory of the chalked whiteness of light.

PHOTOGRAPHS

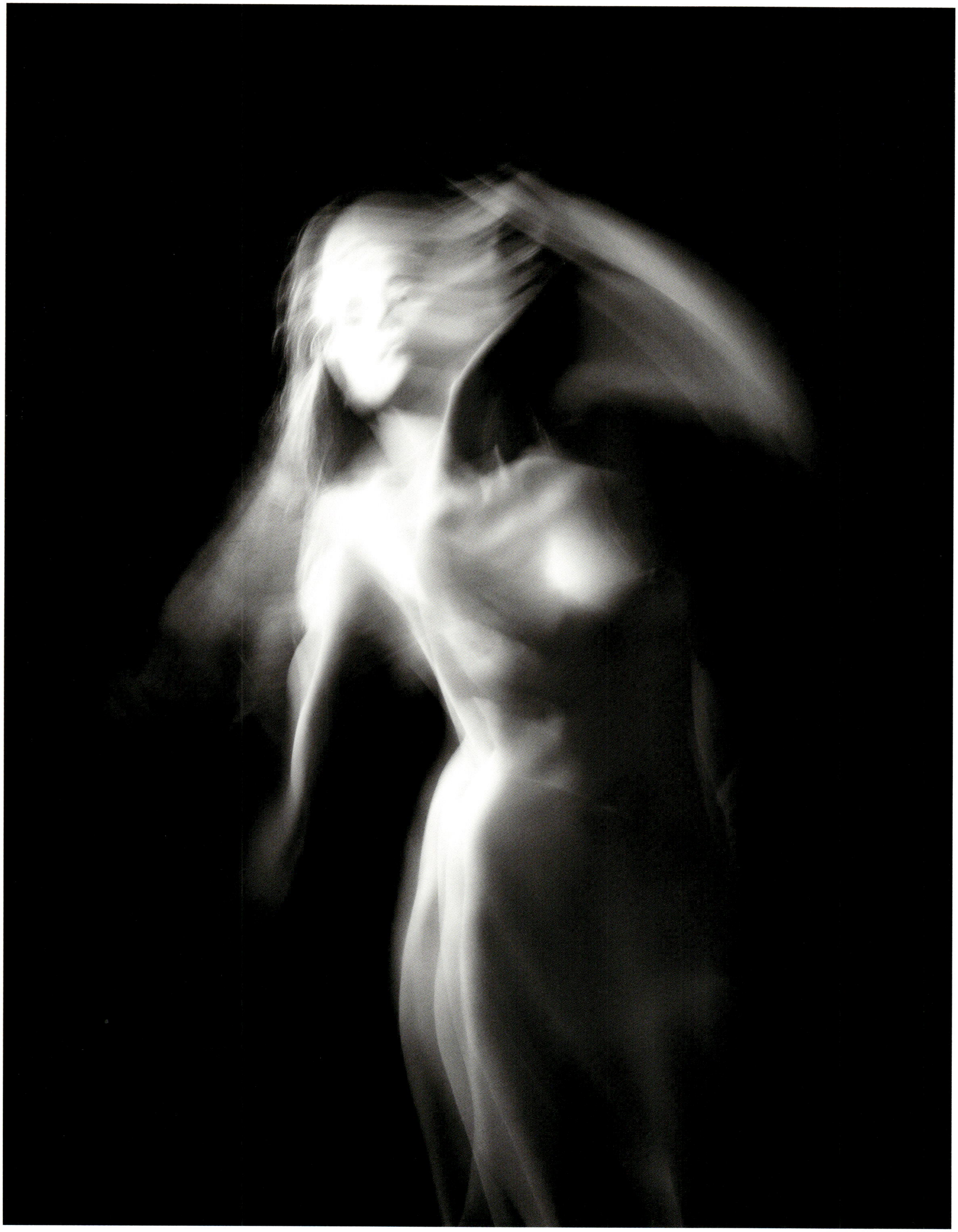

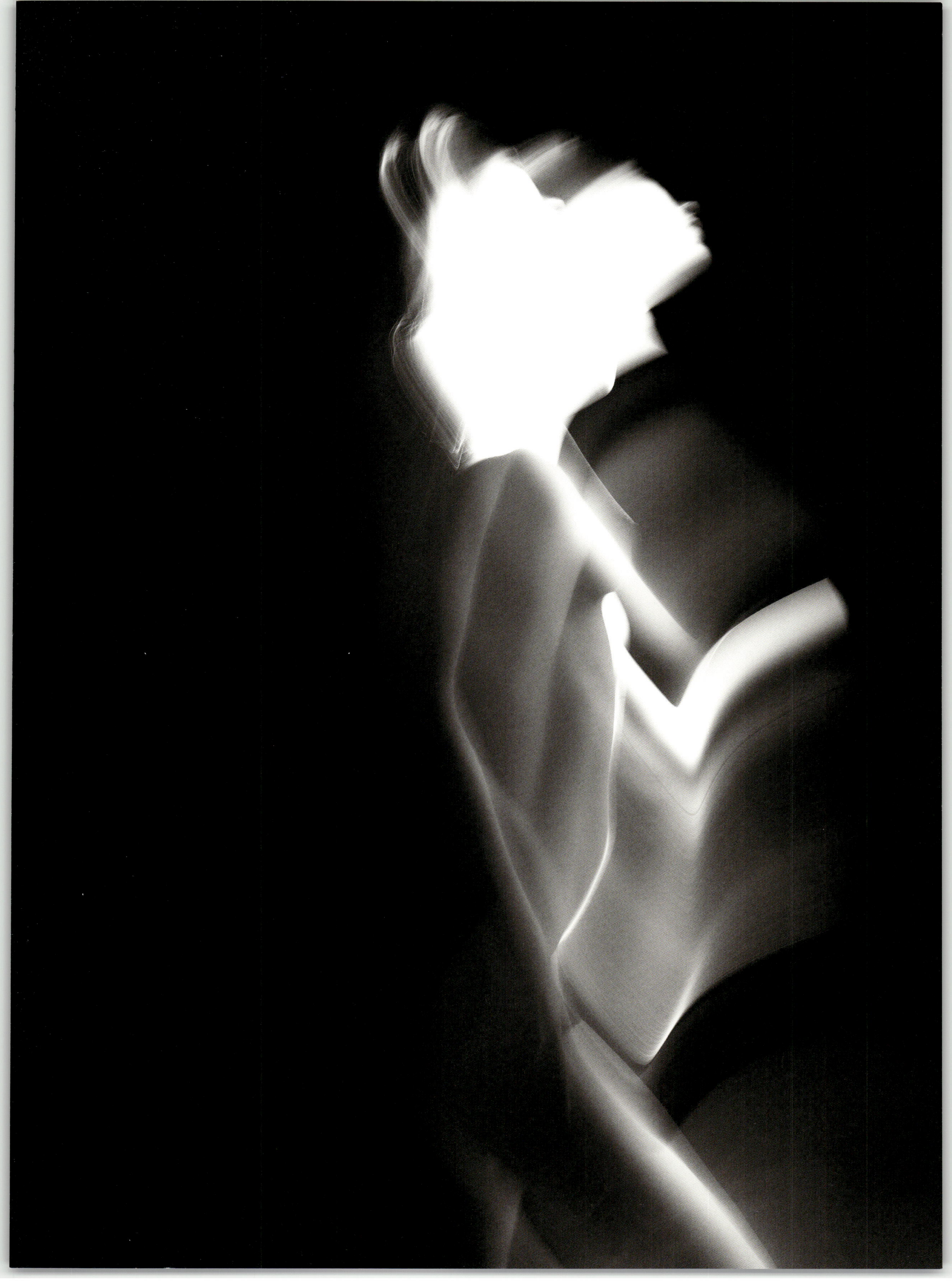

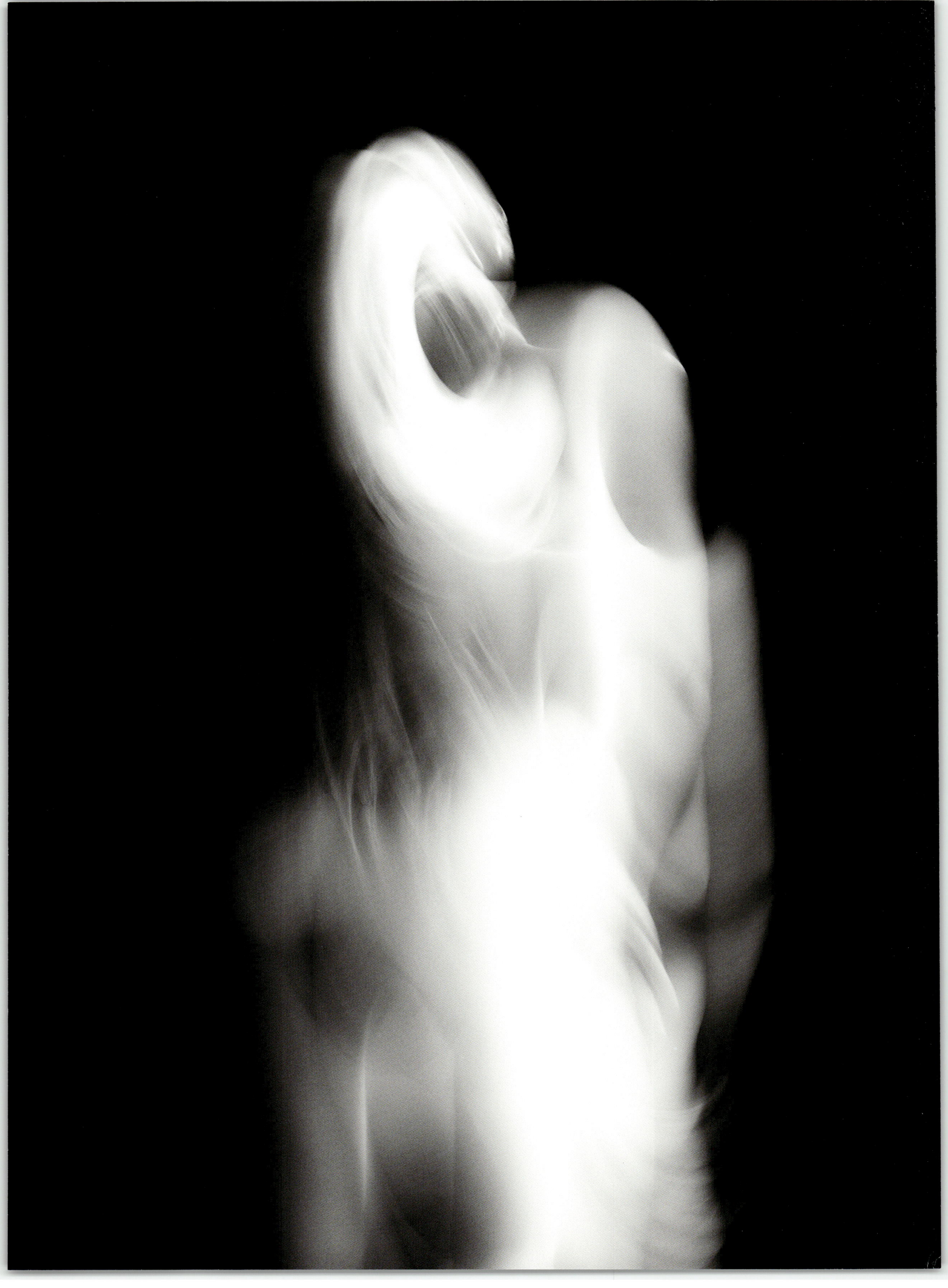

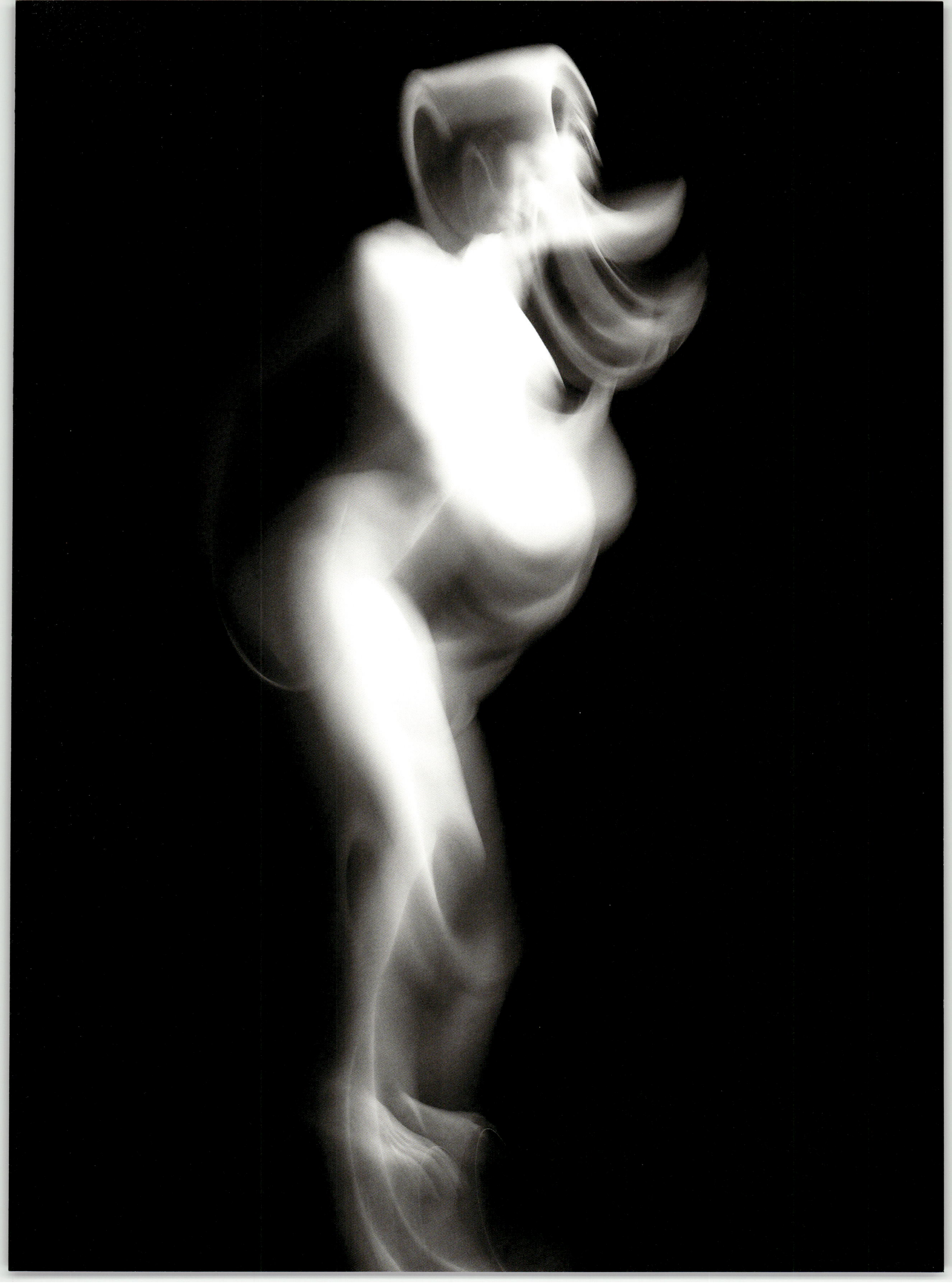

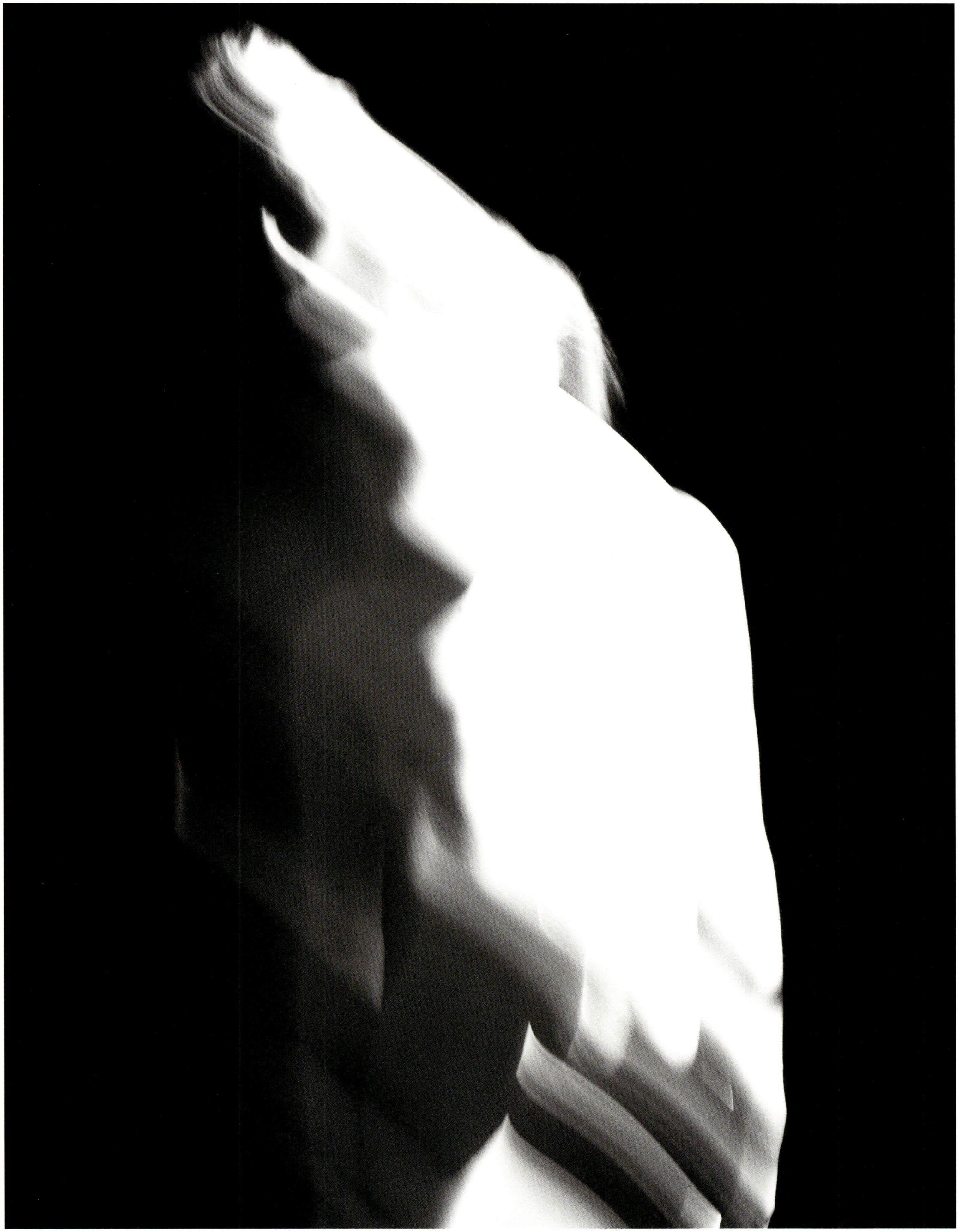

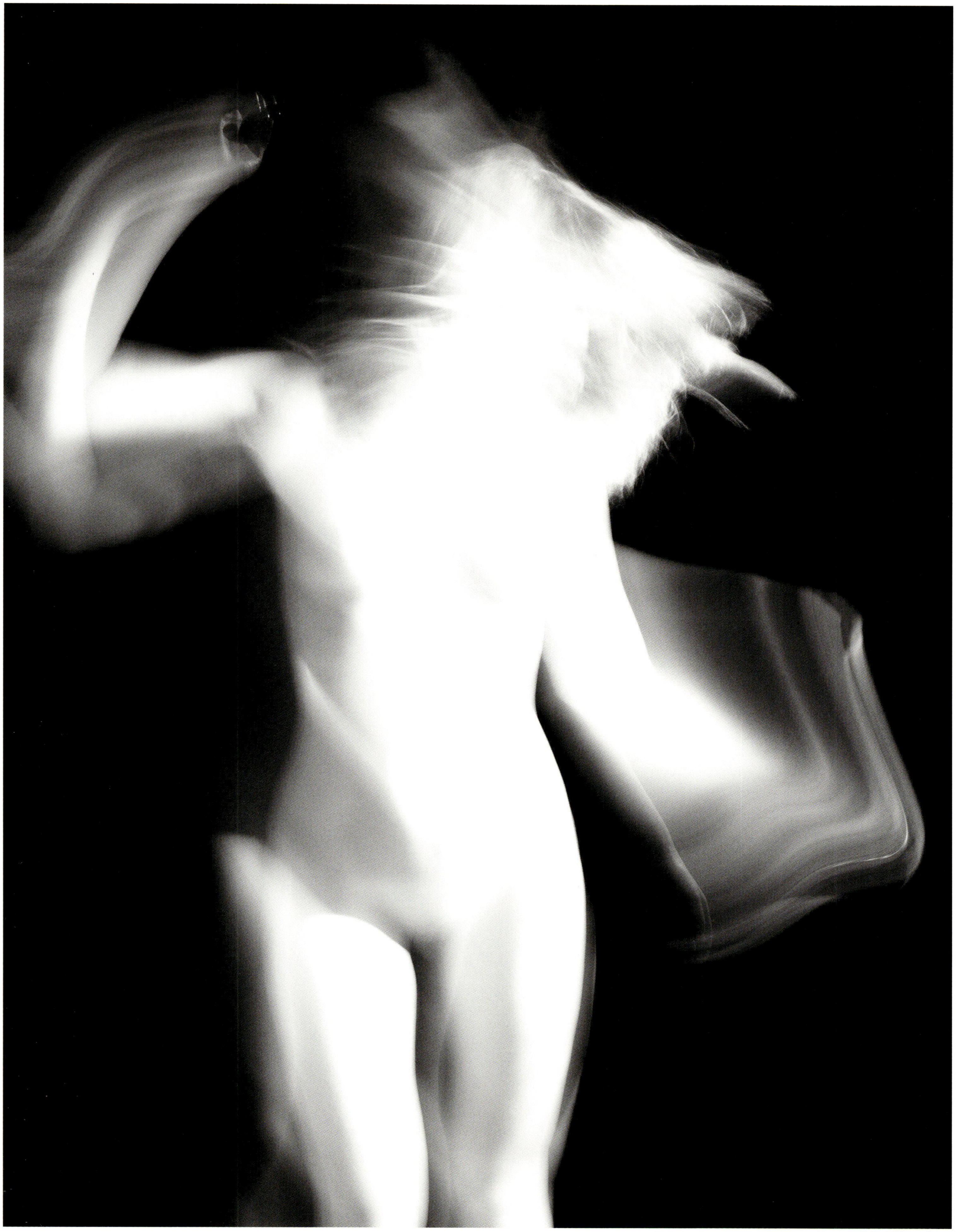

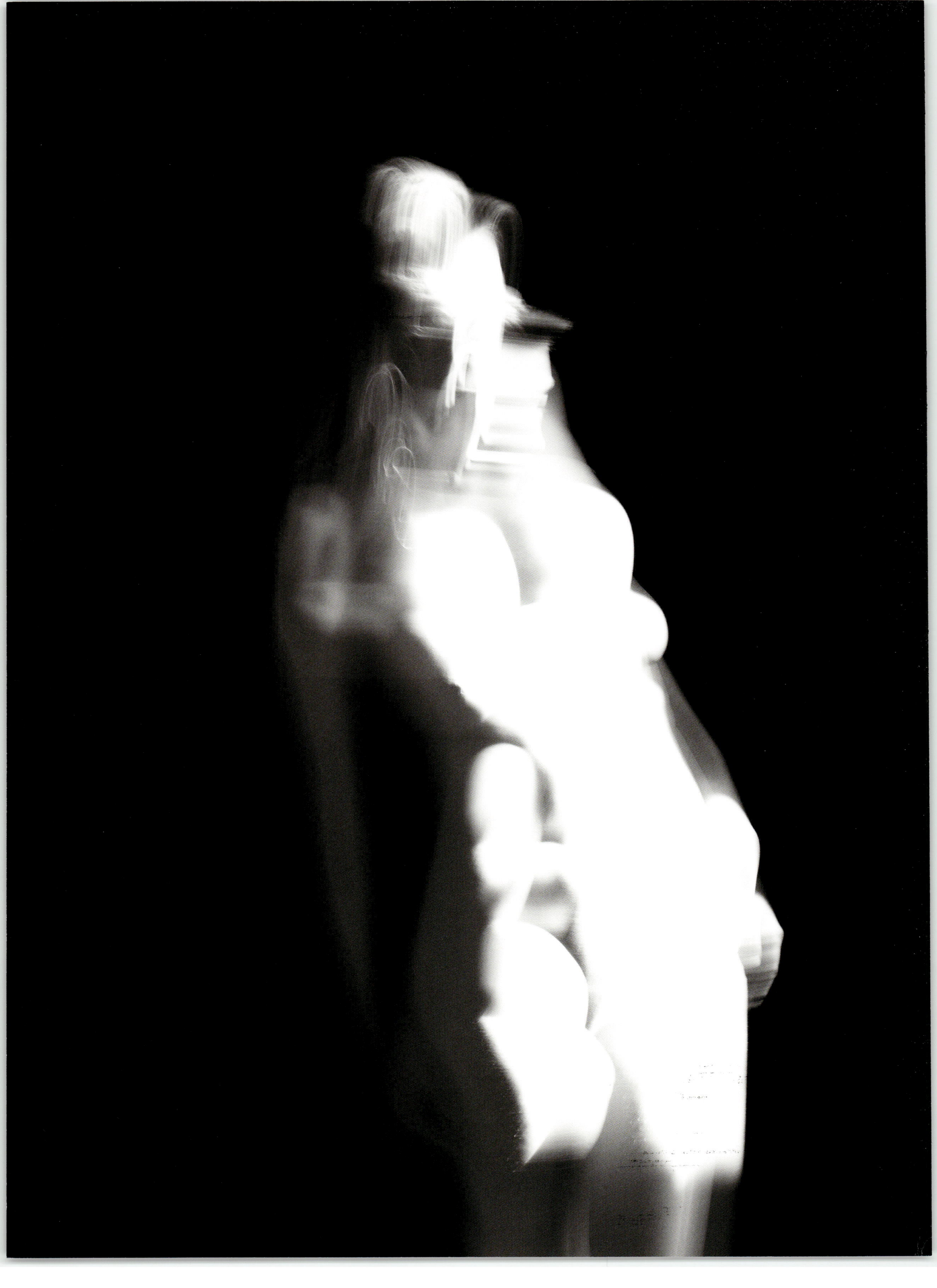

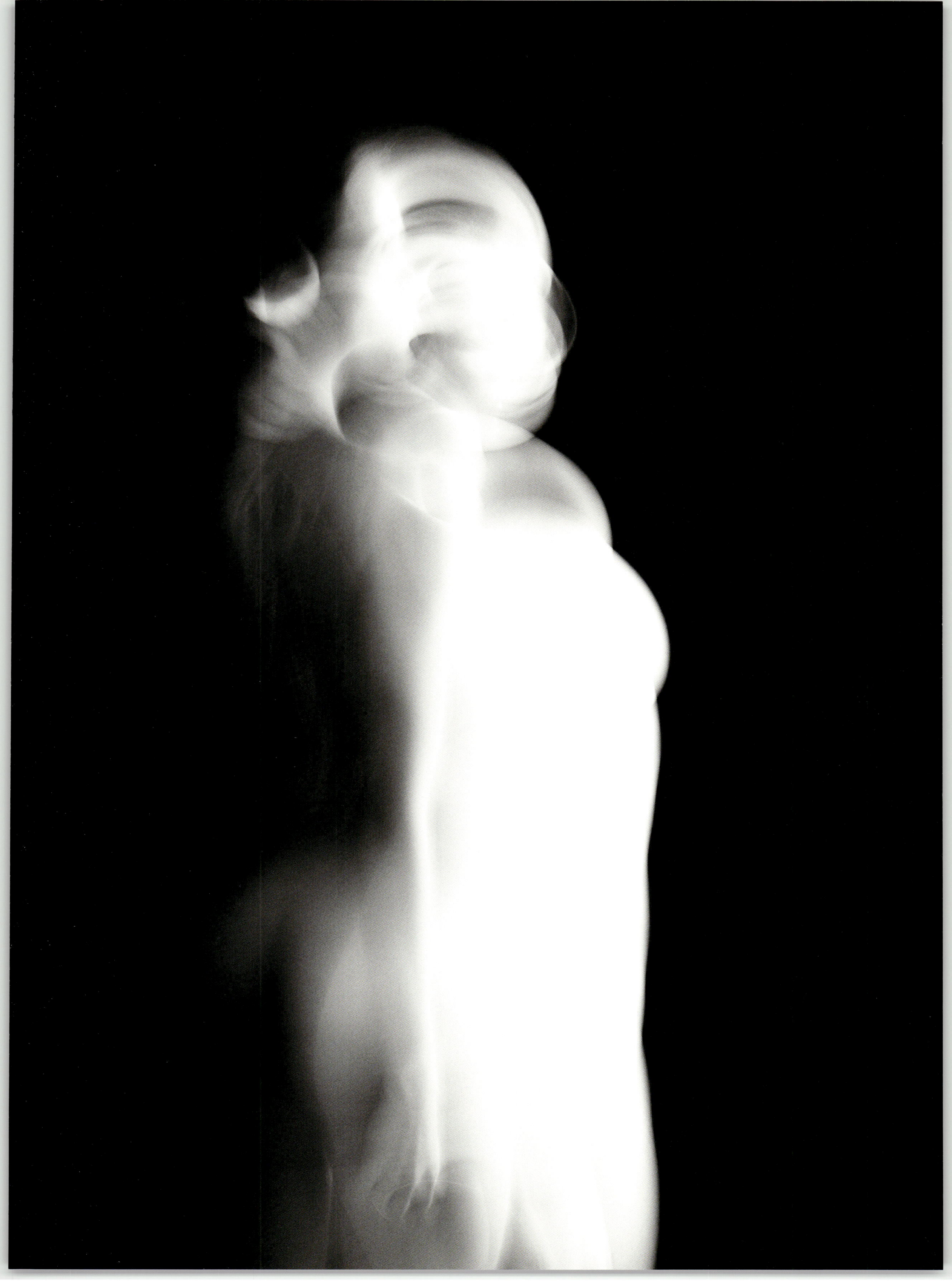

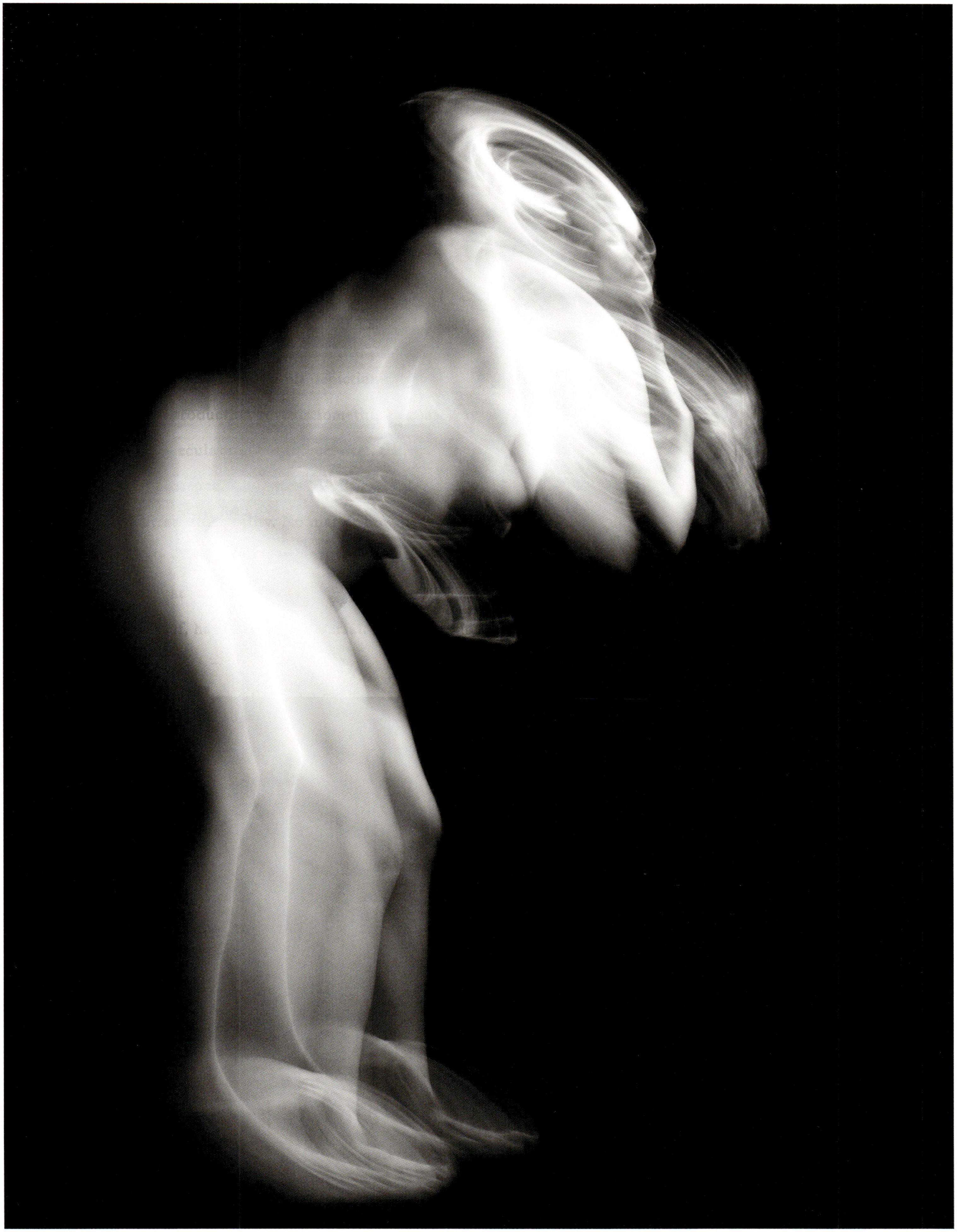

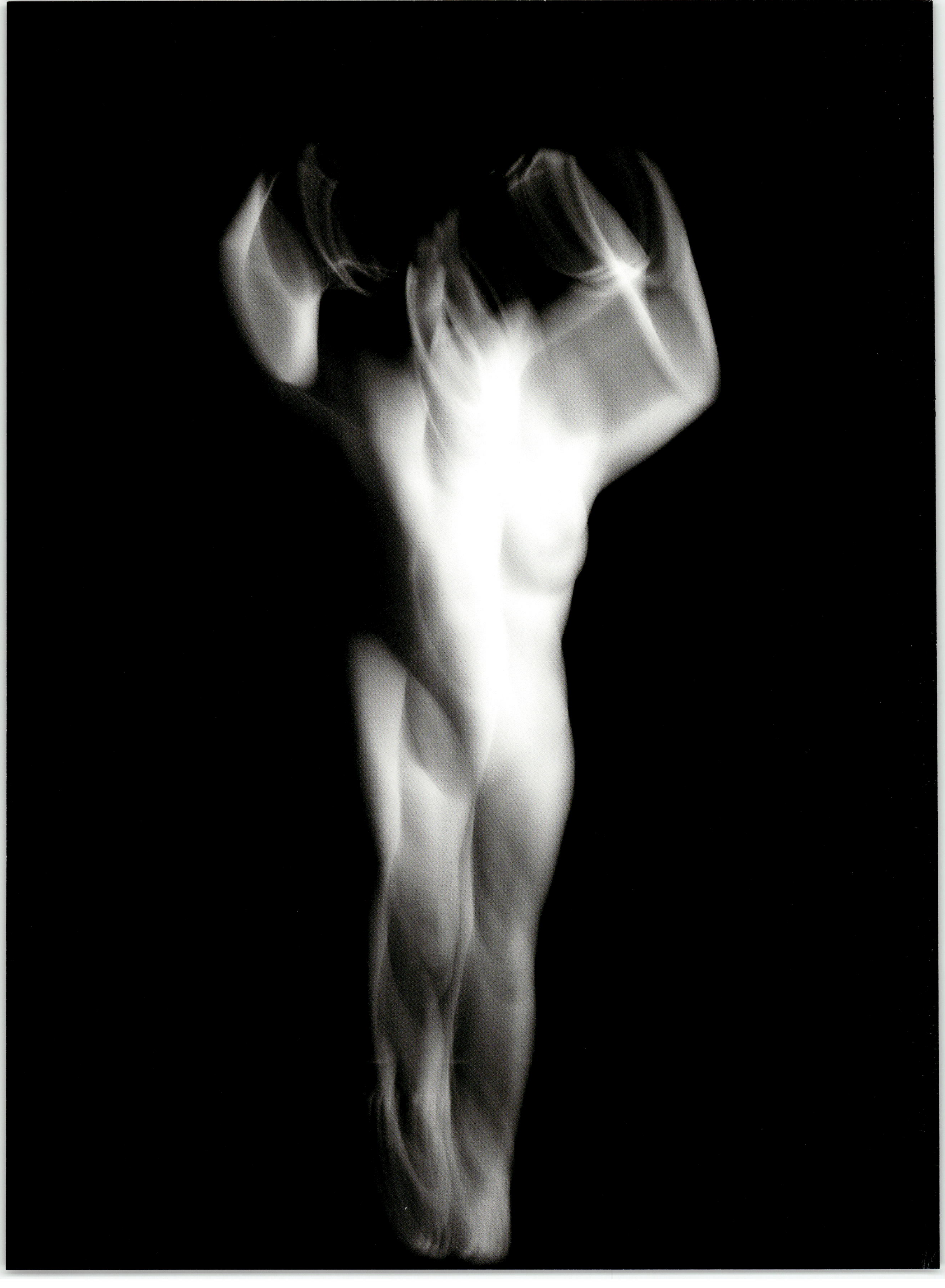

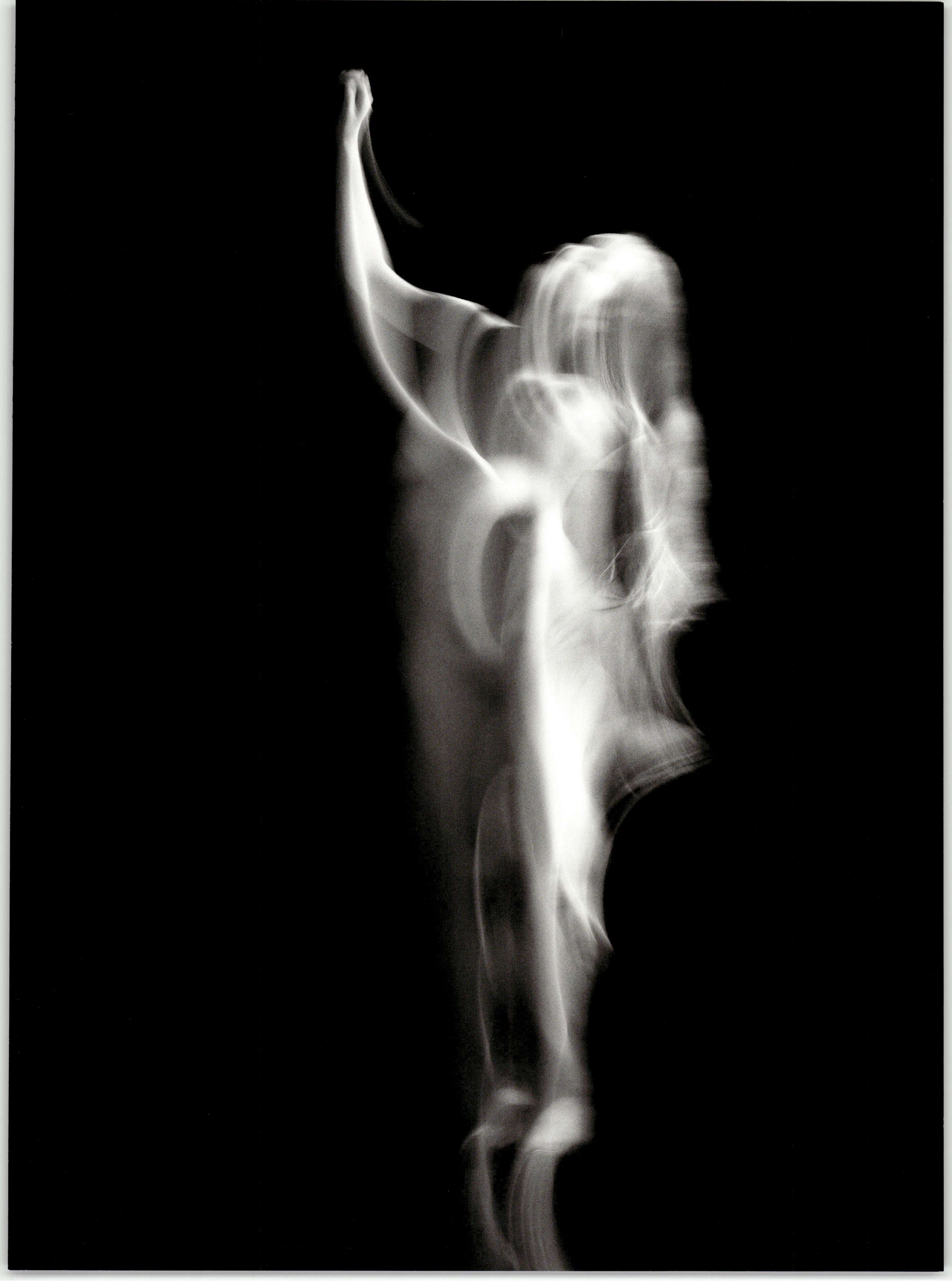

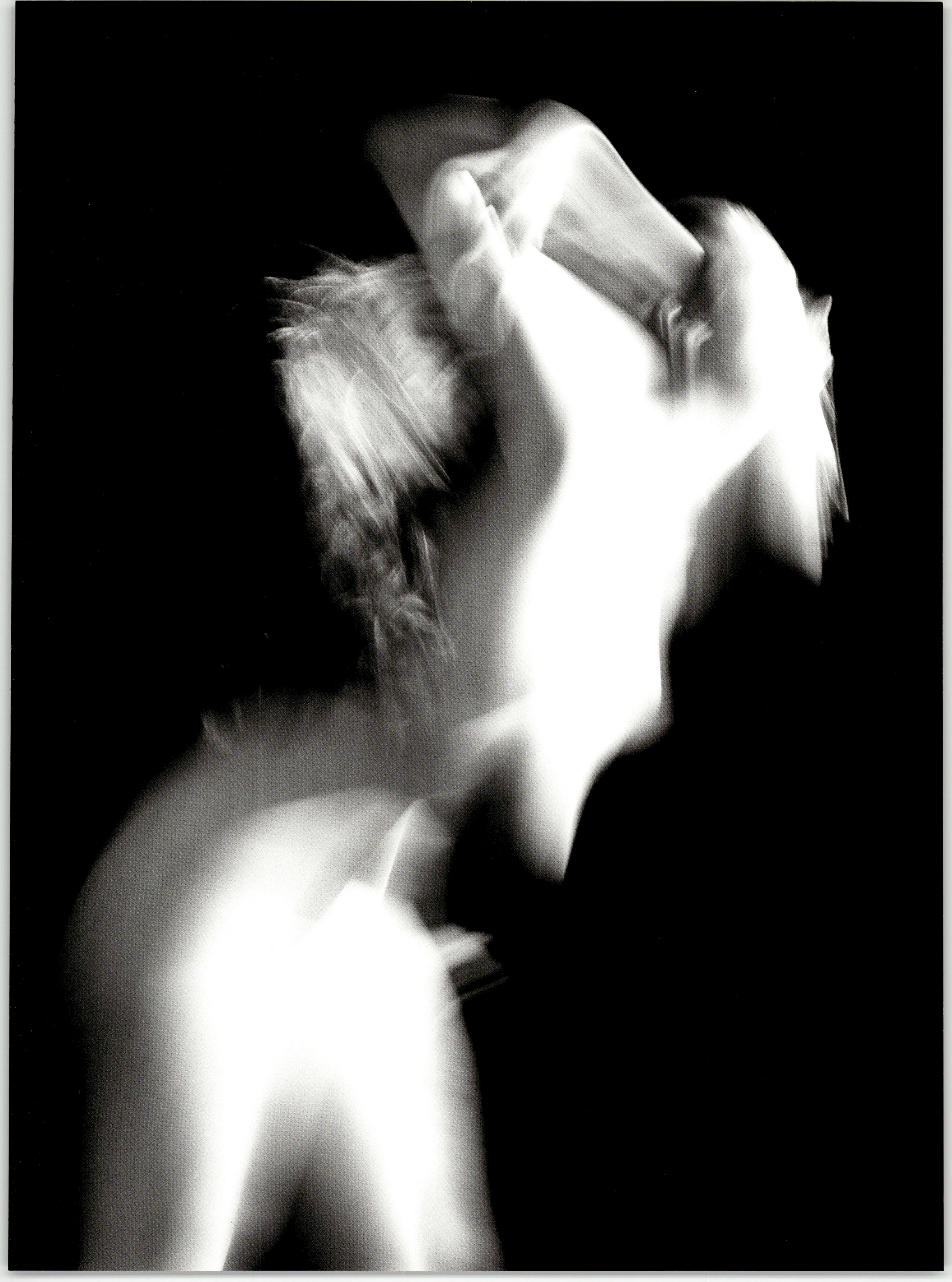

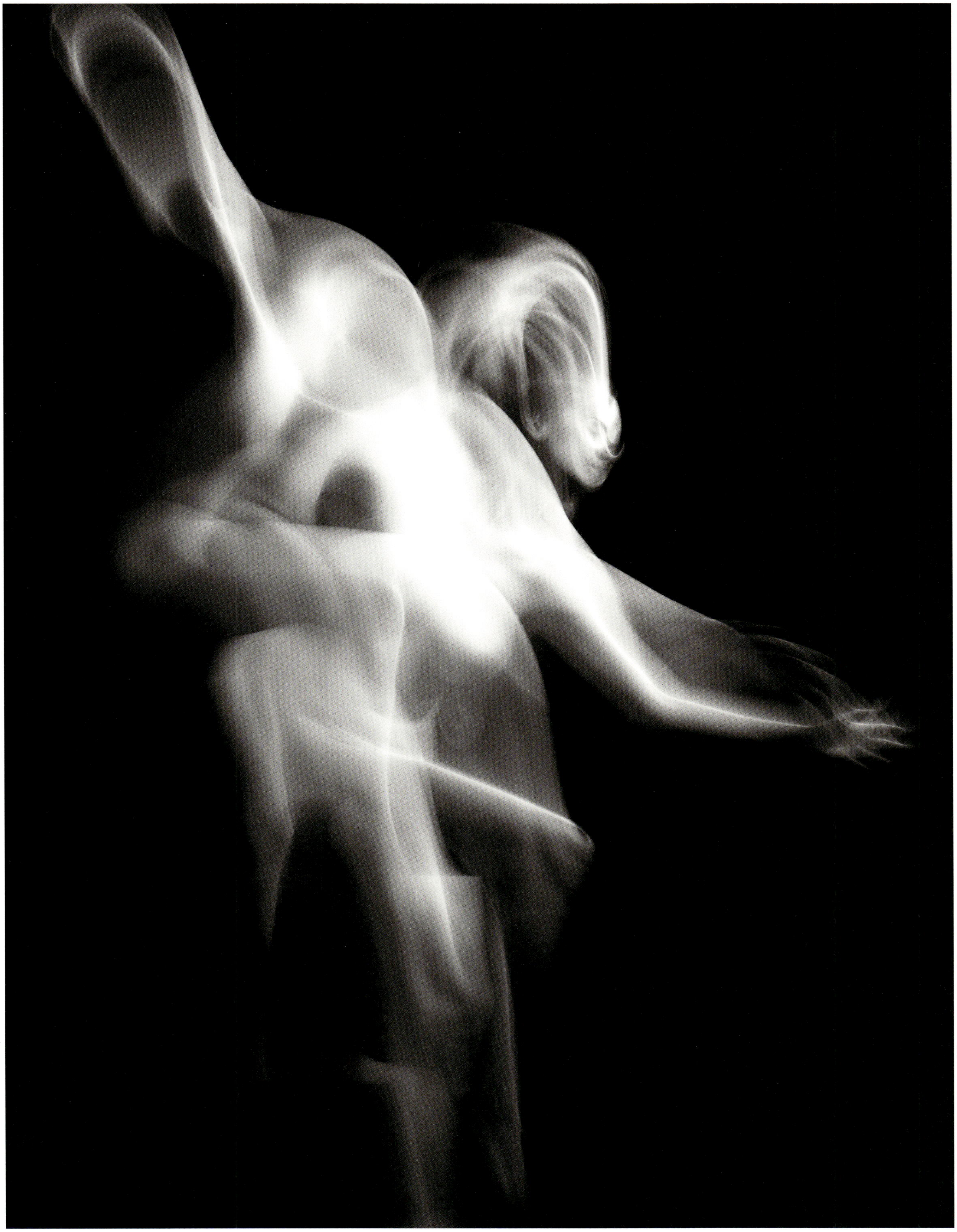

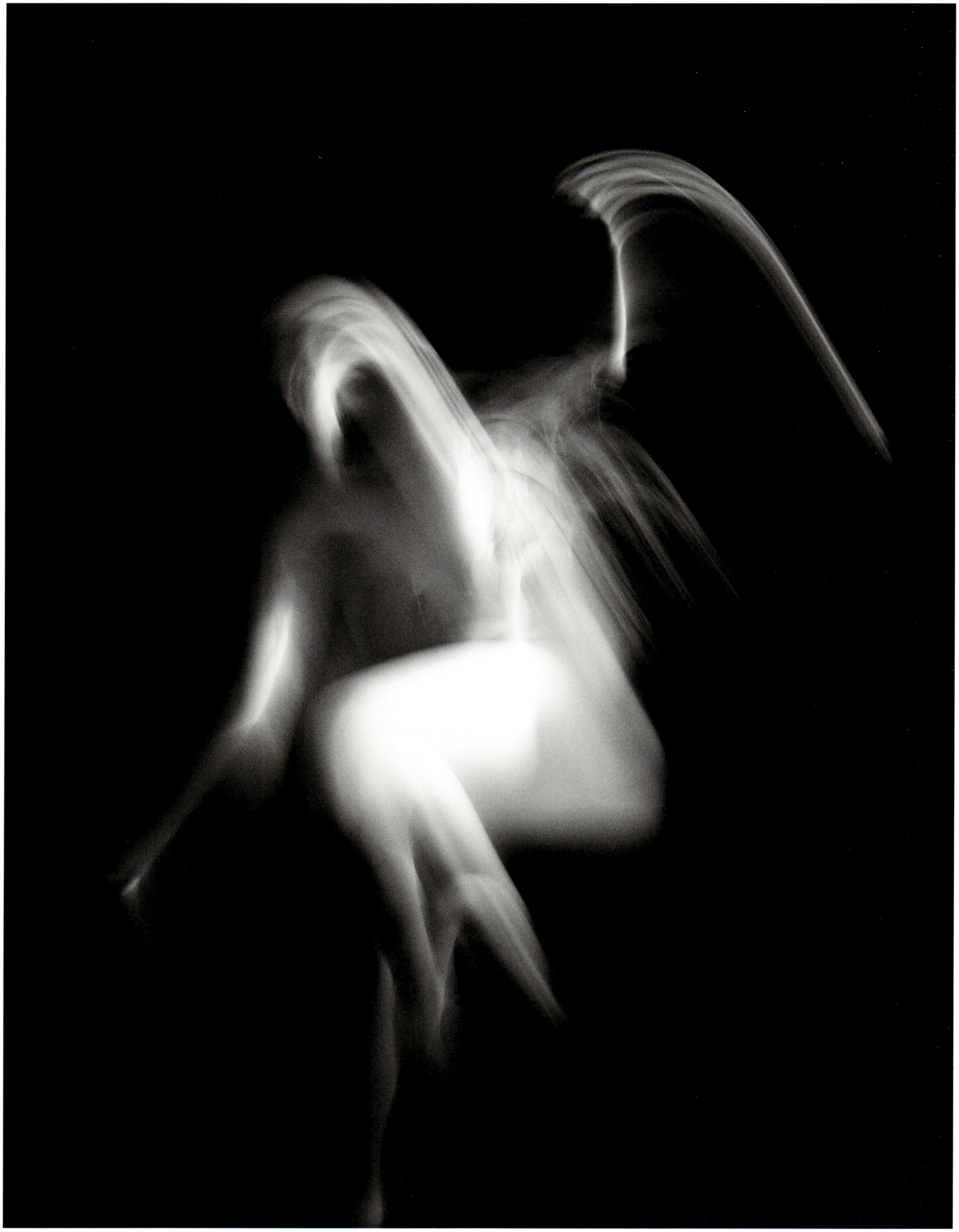

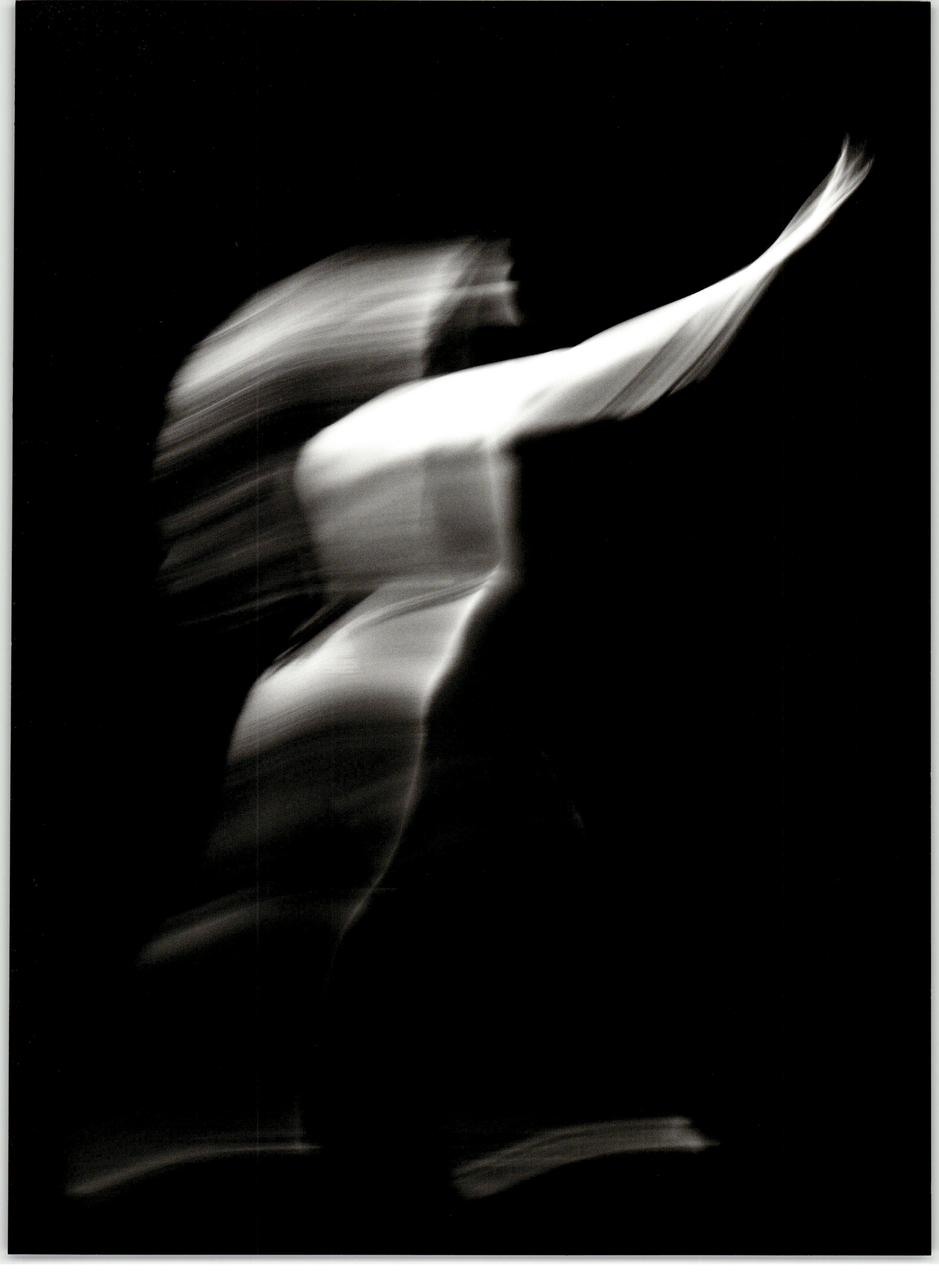

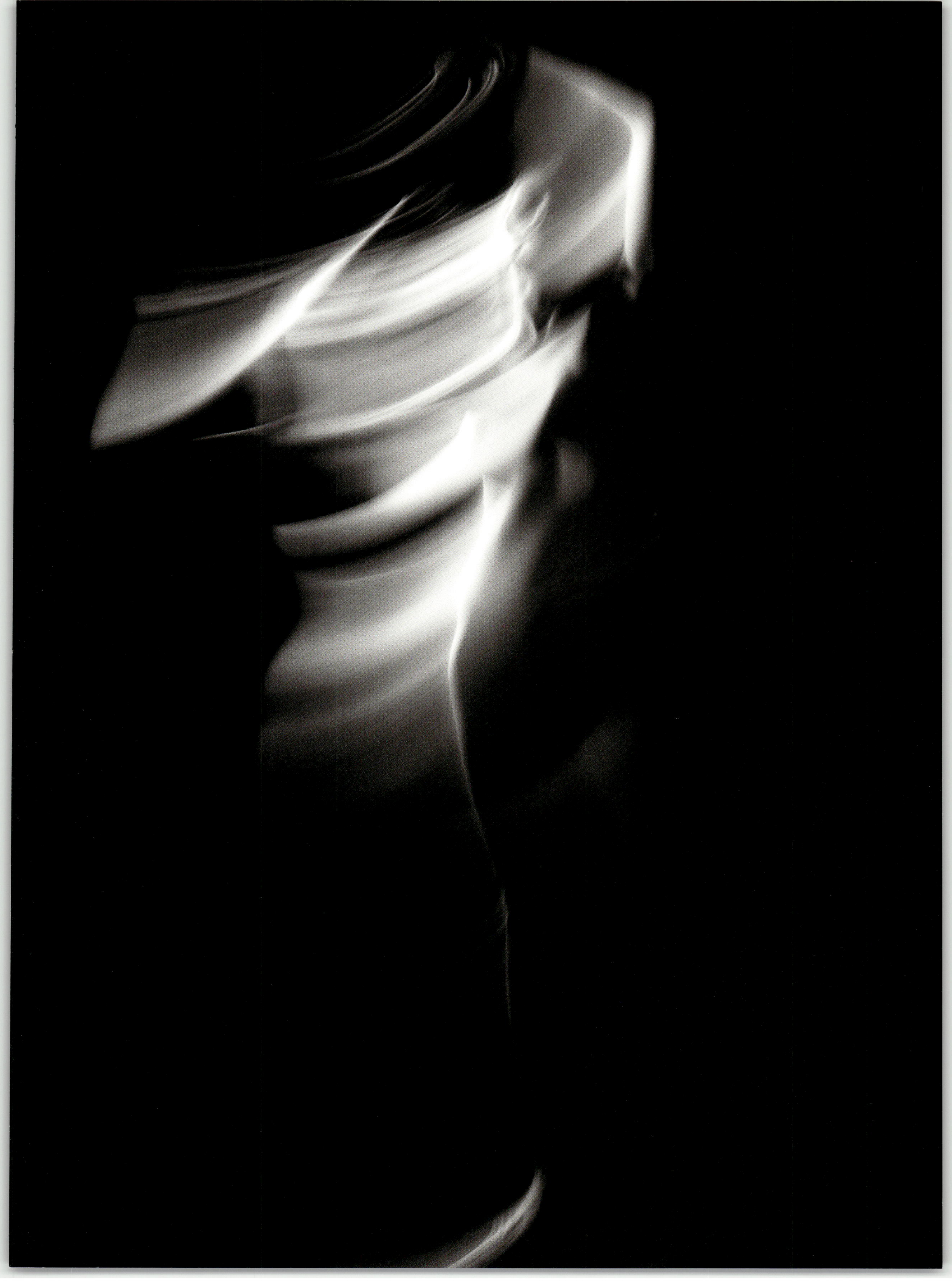

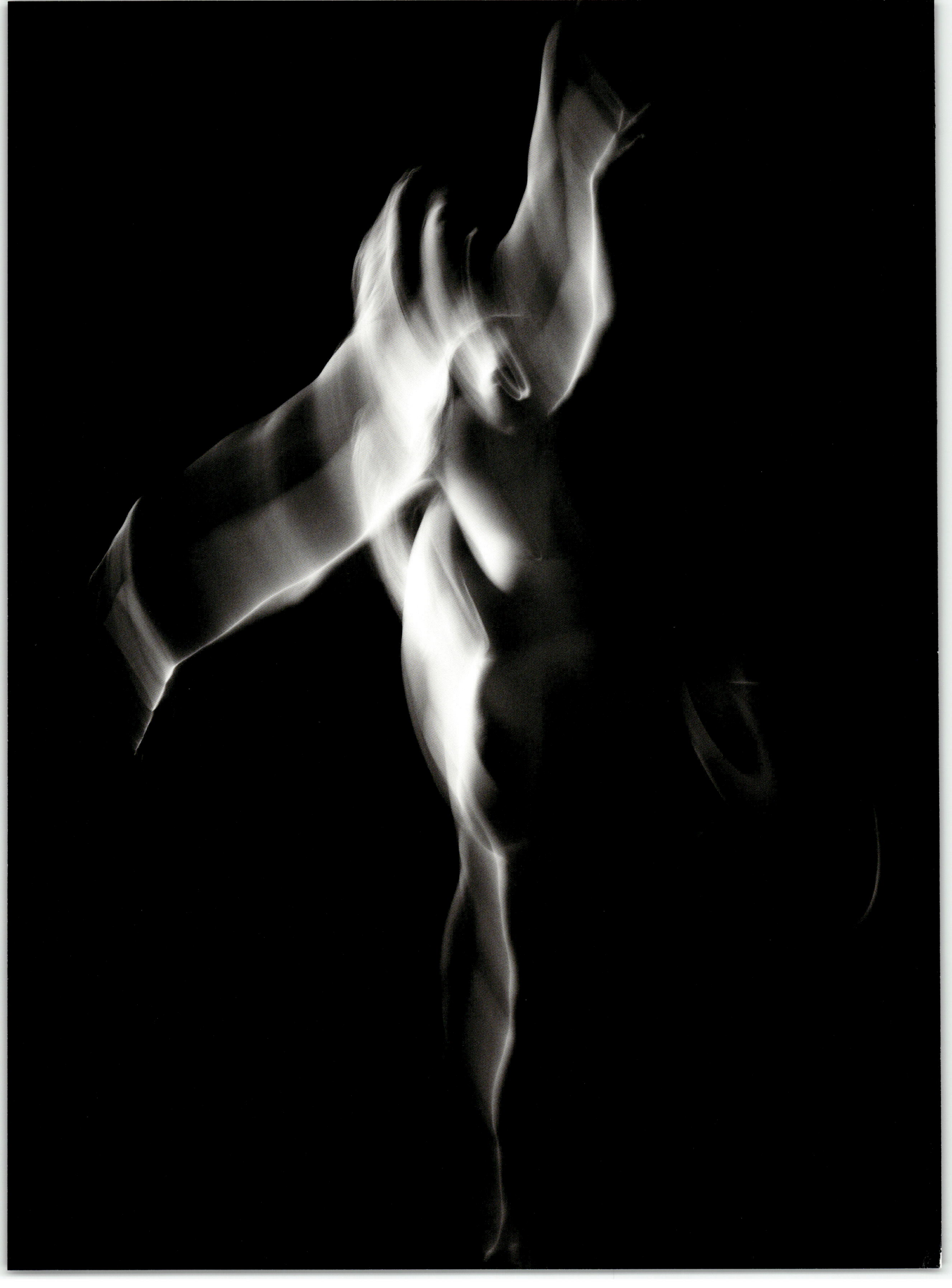

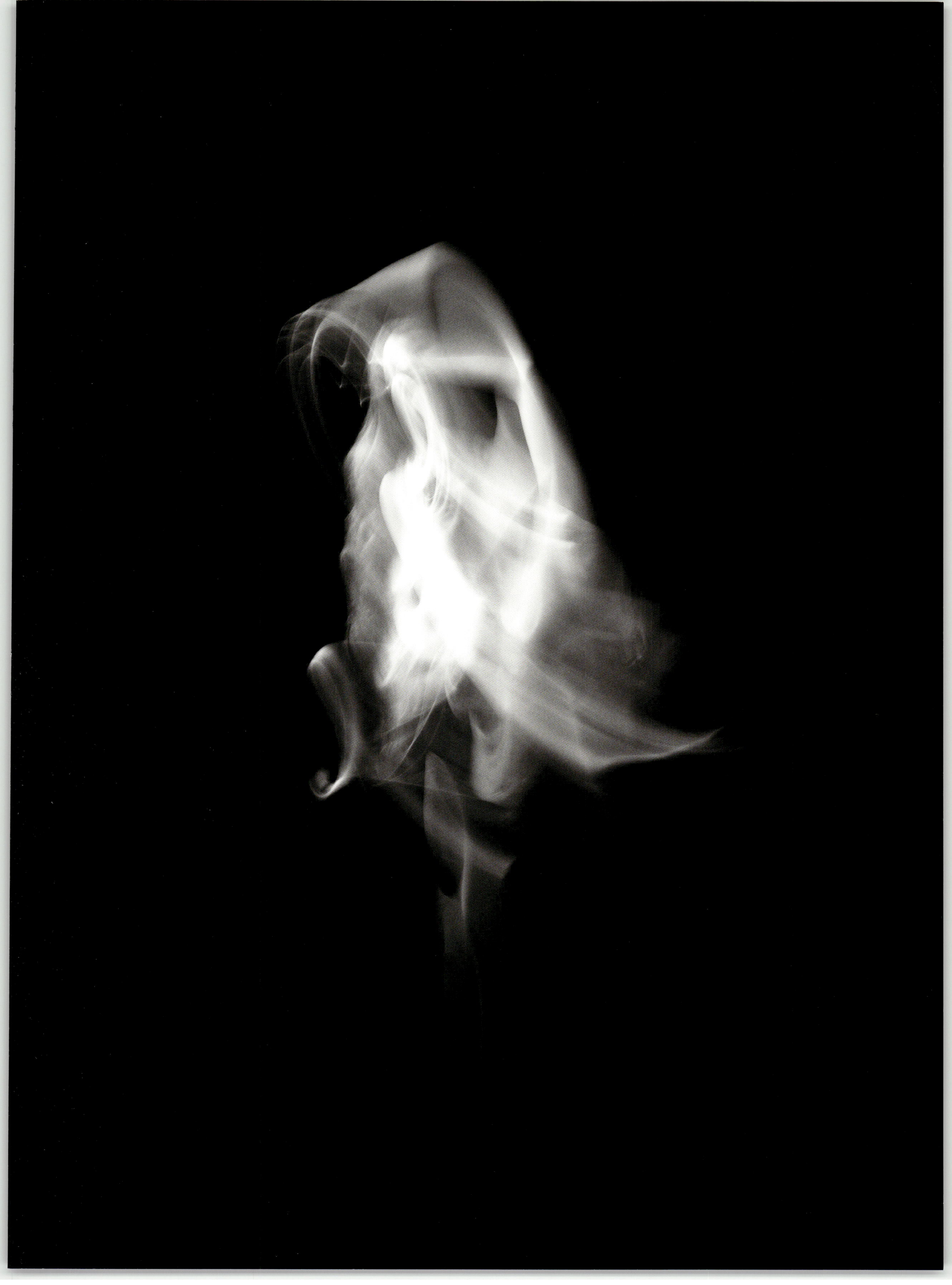

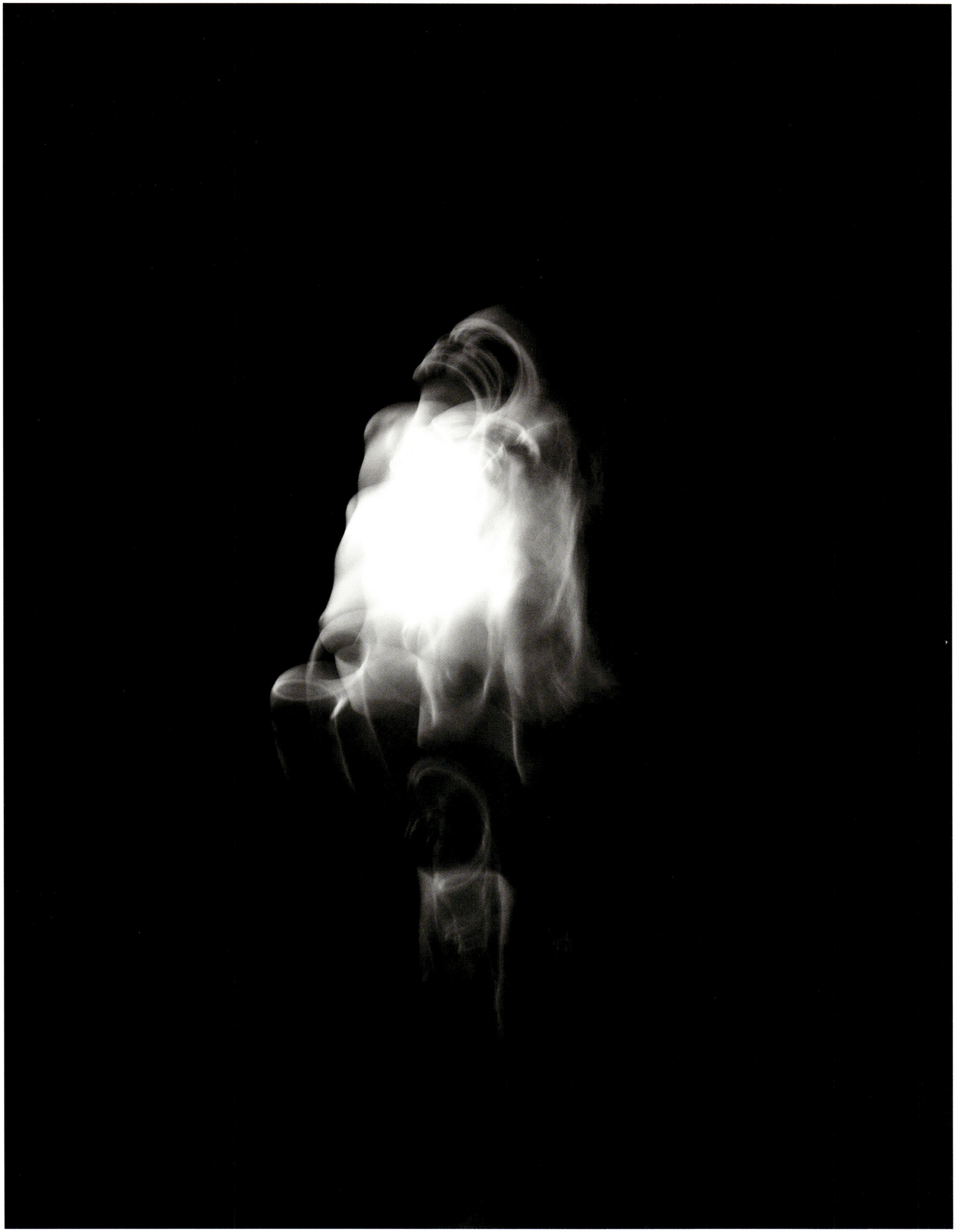

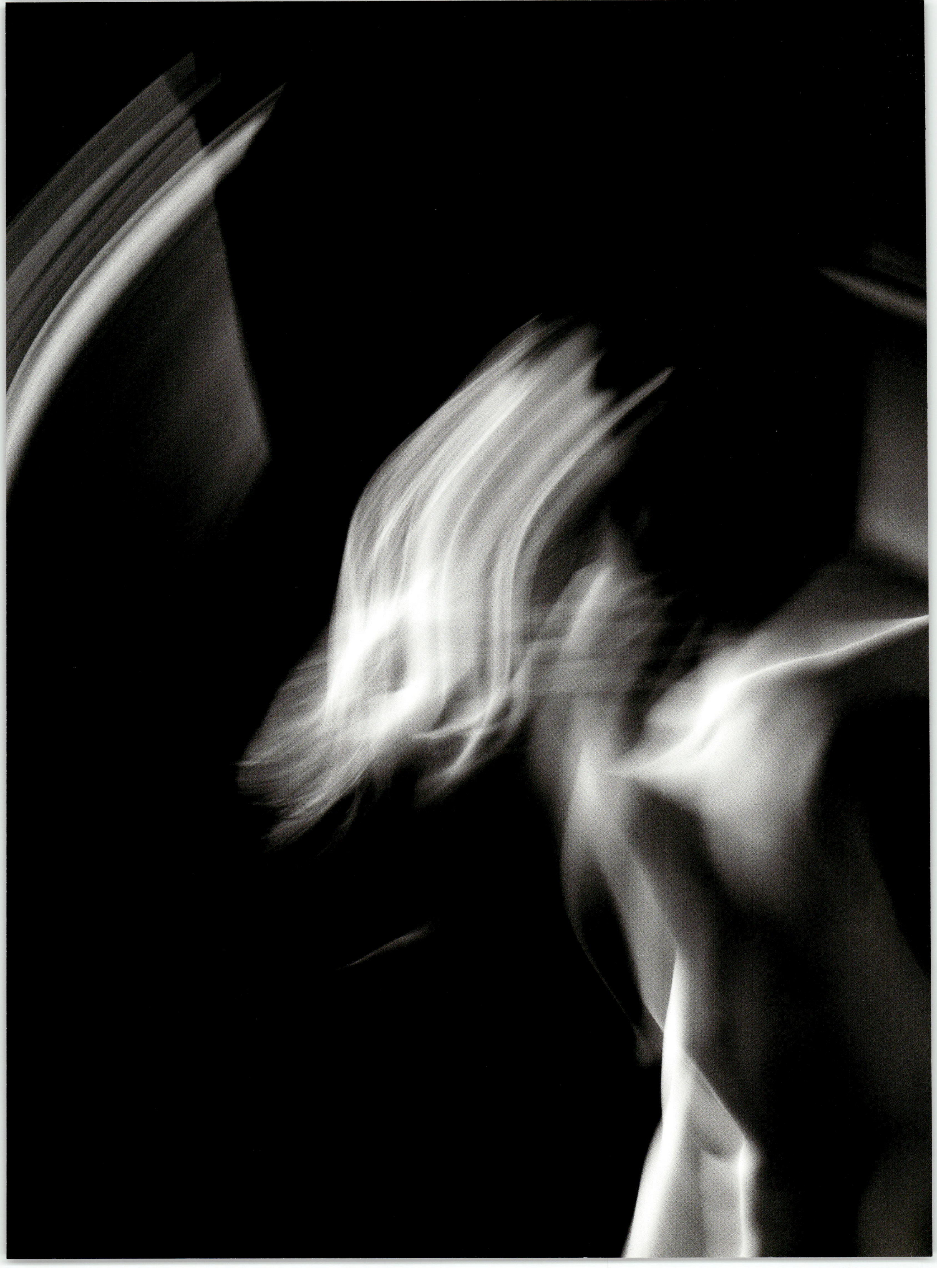

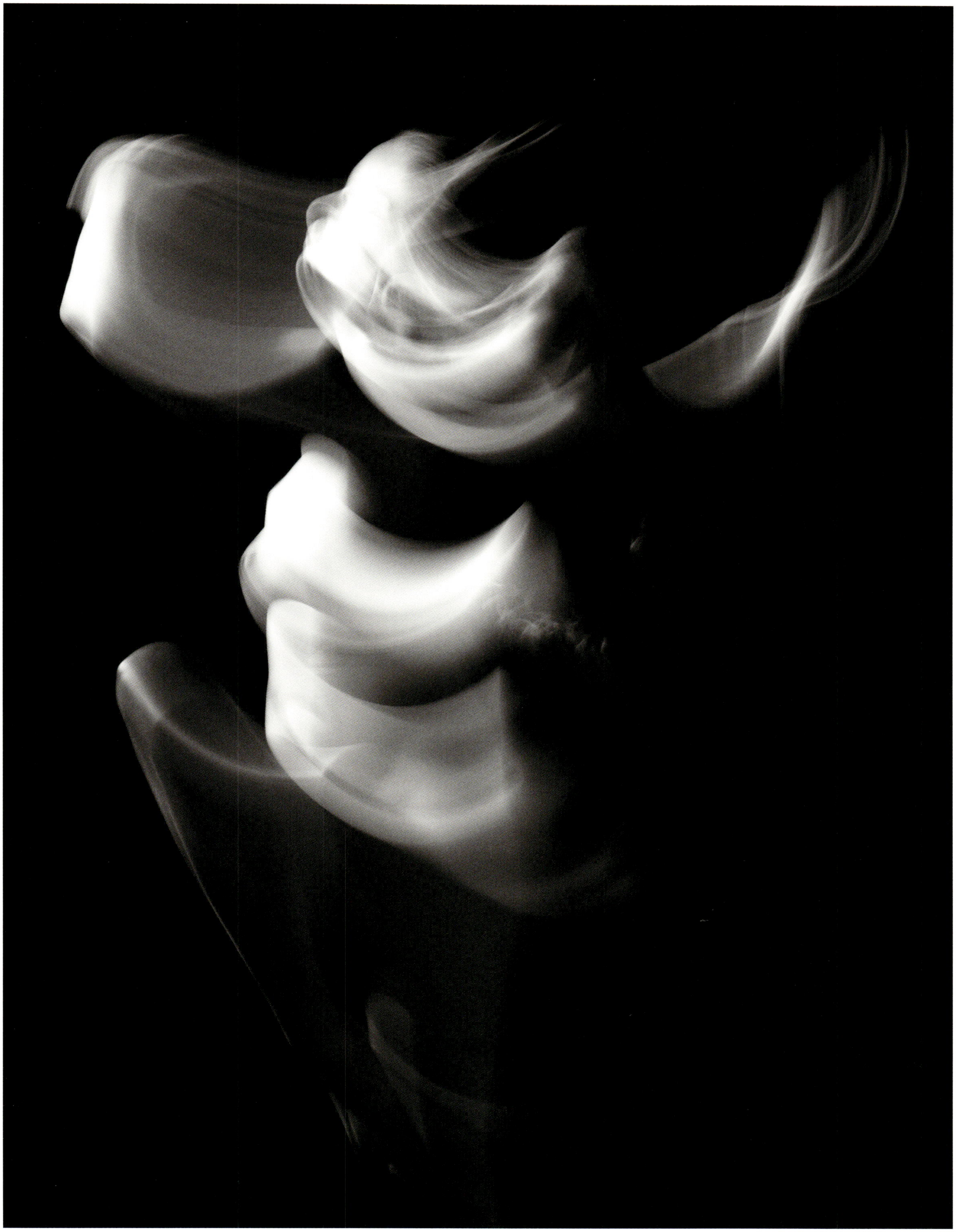

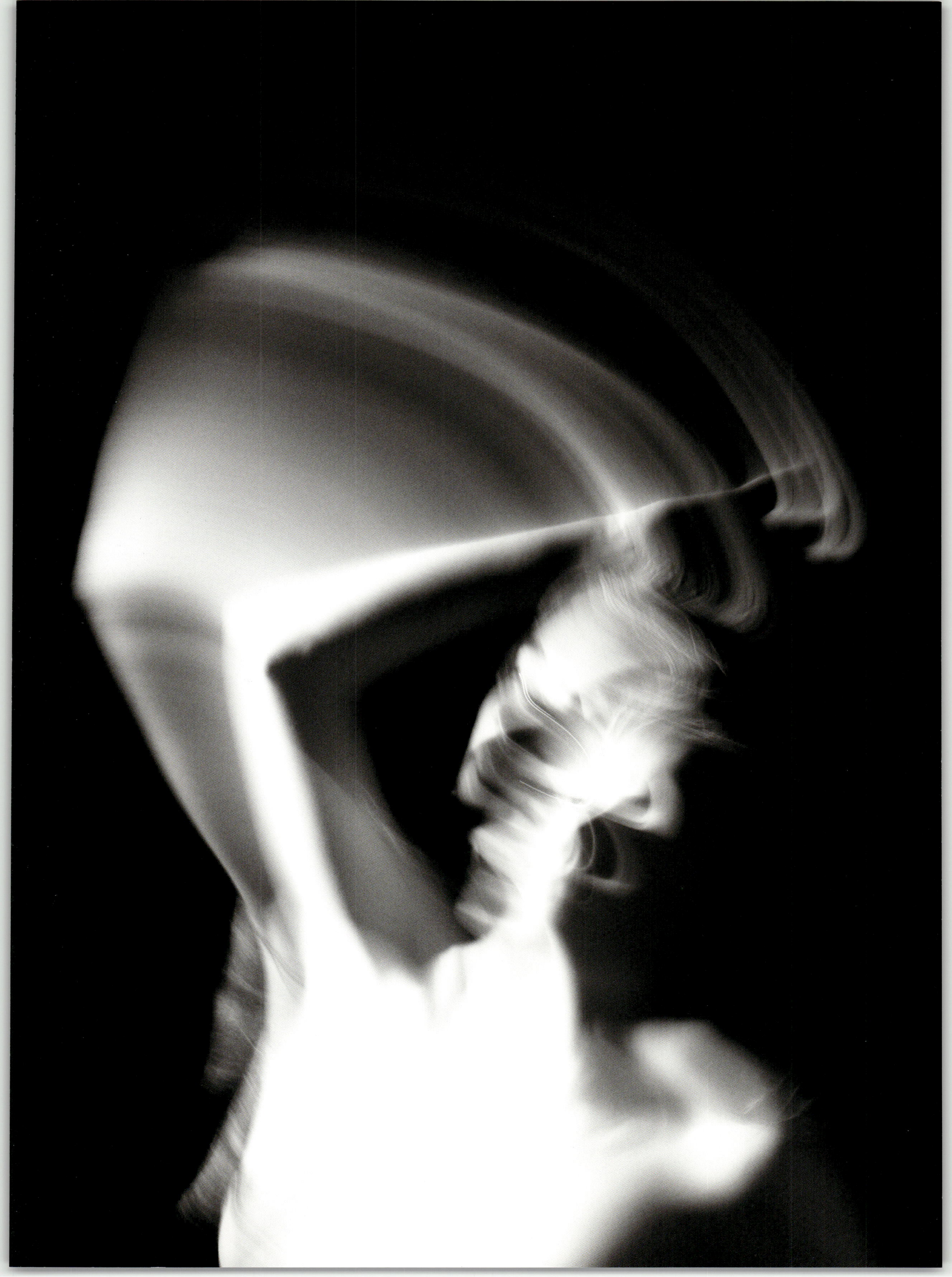

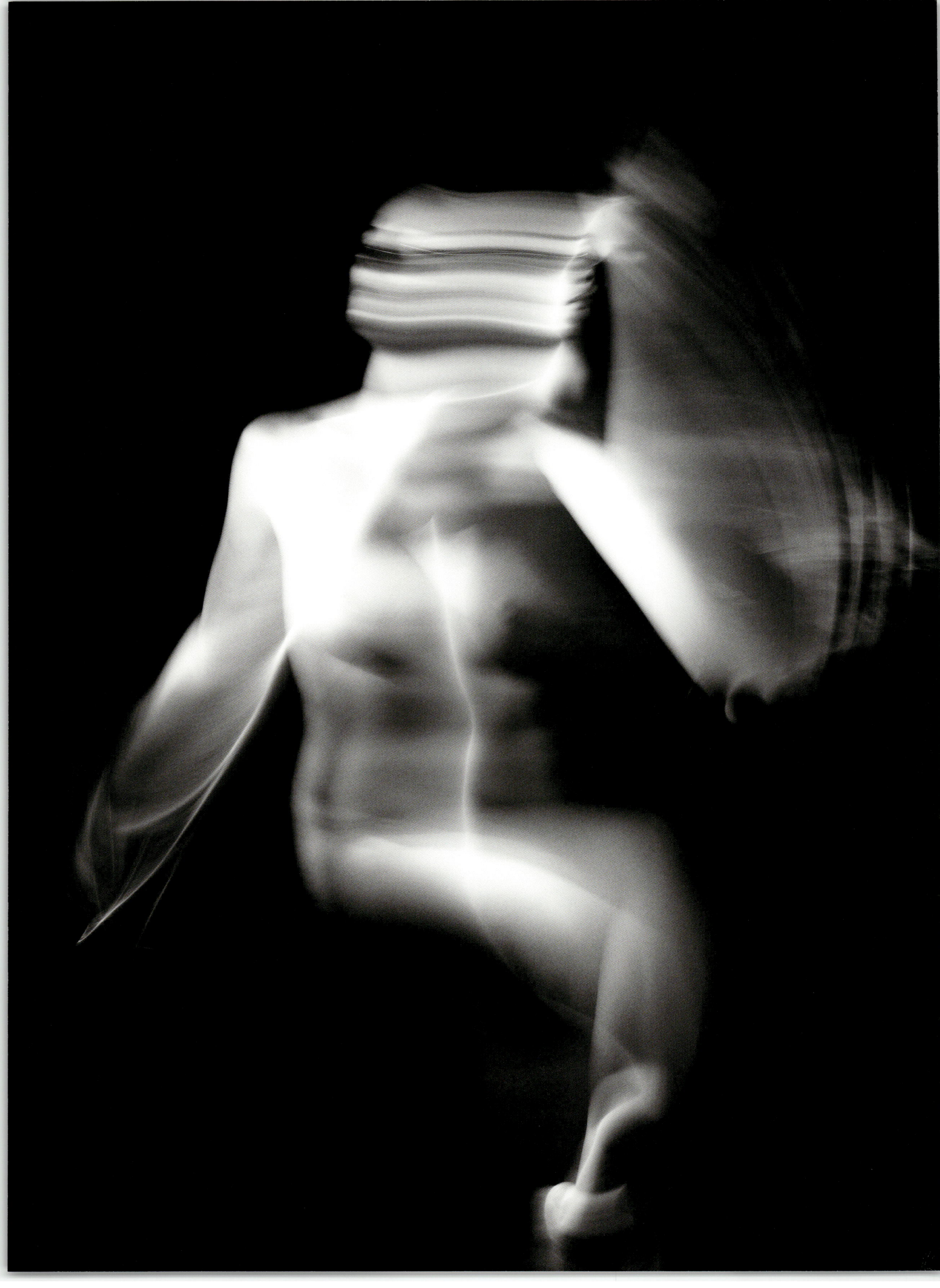

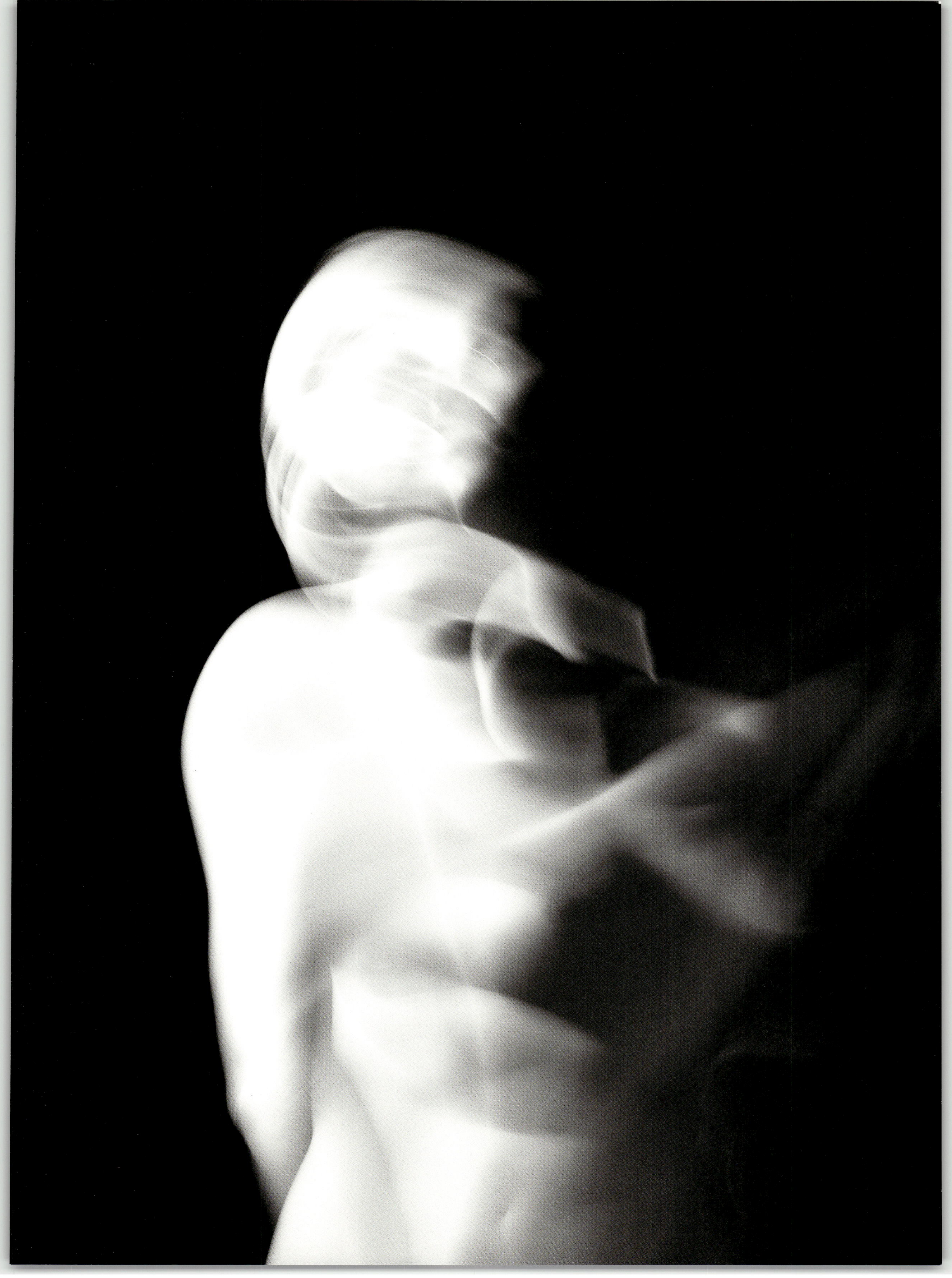

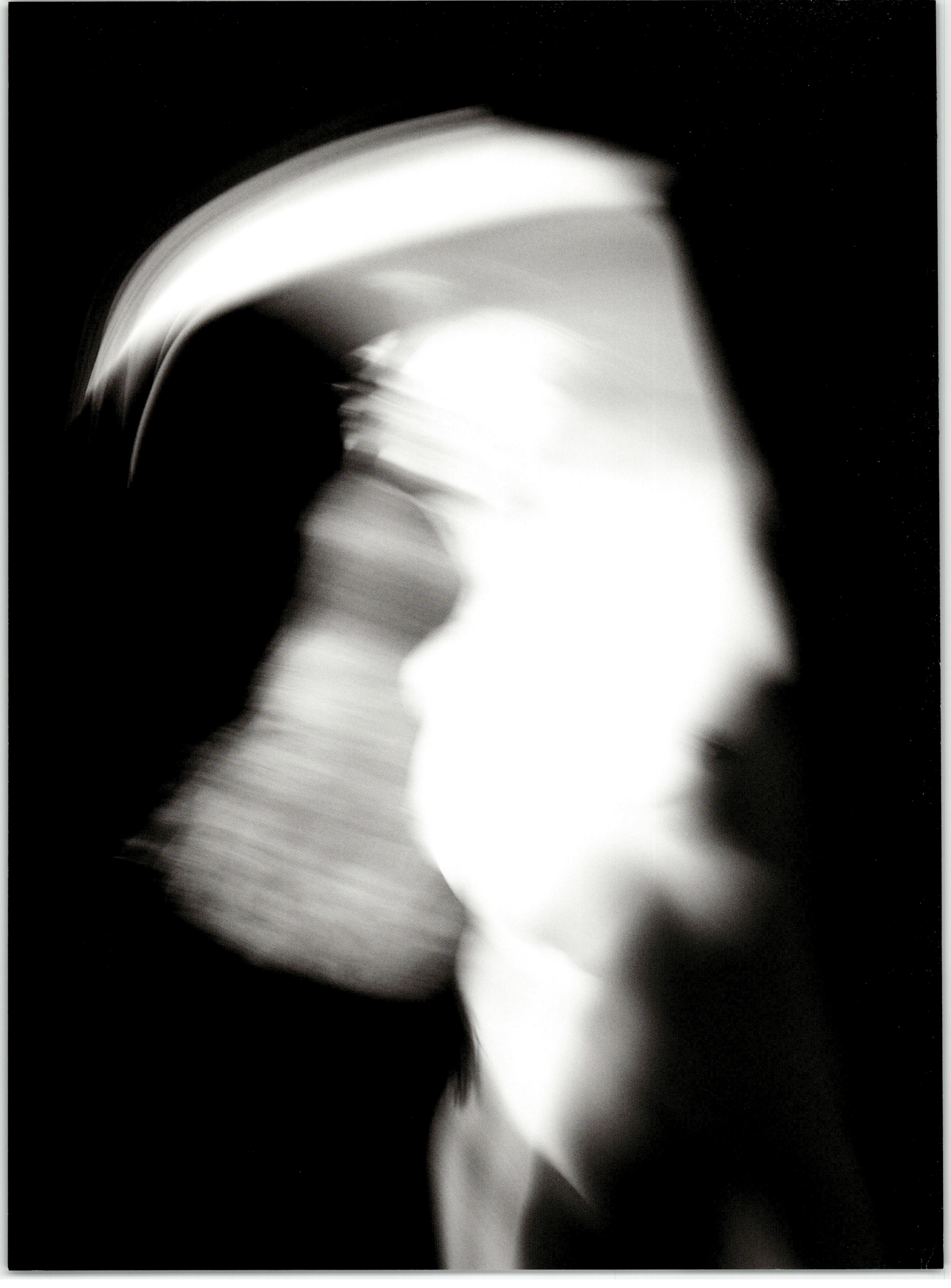

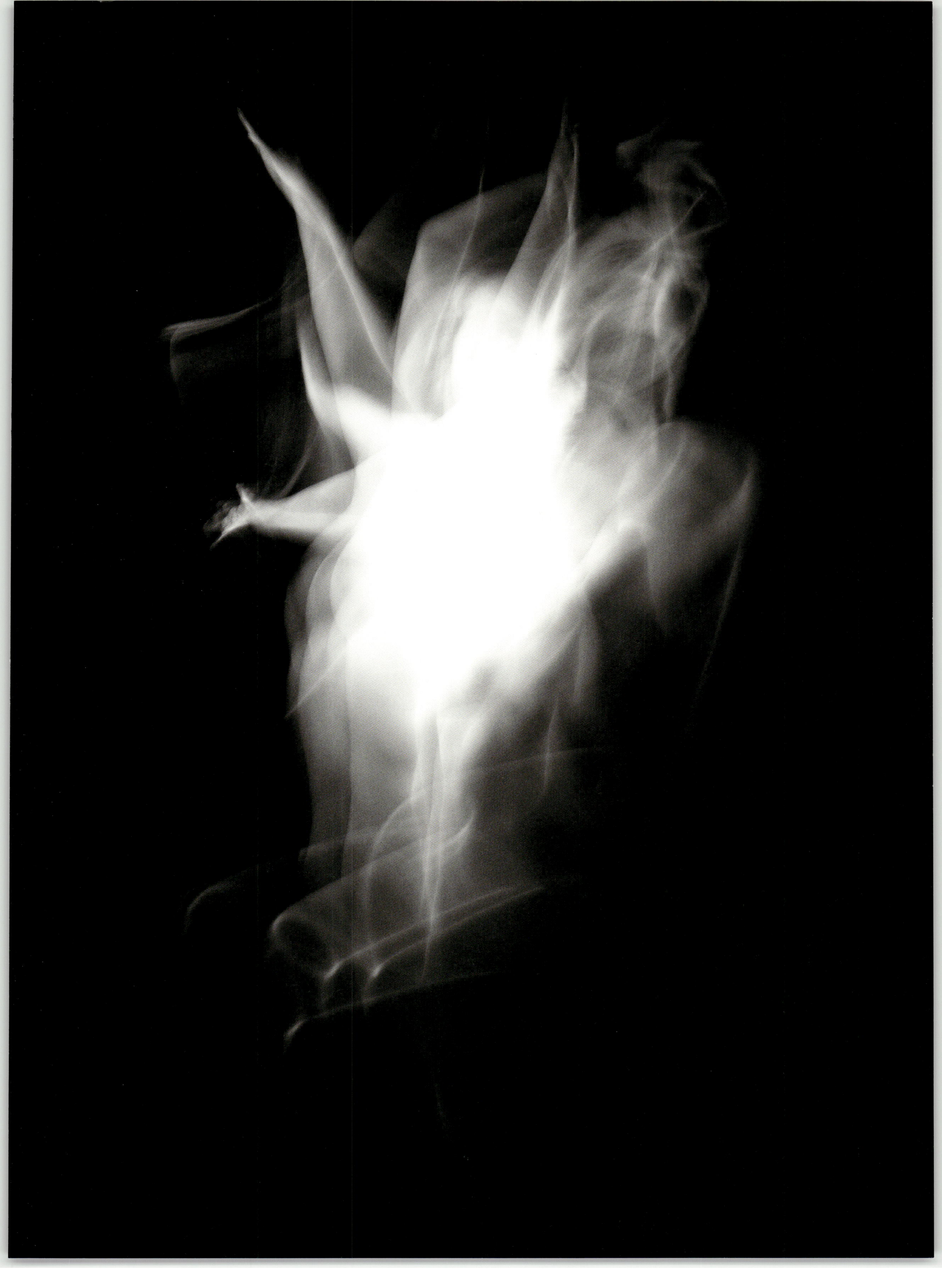

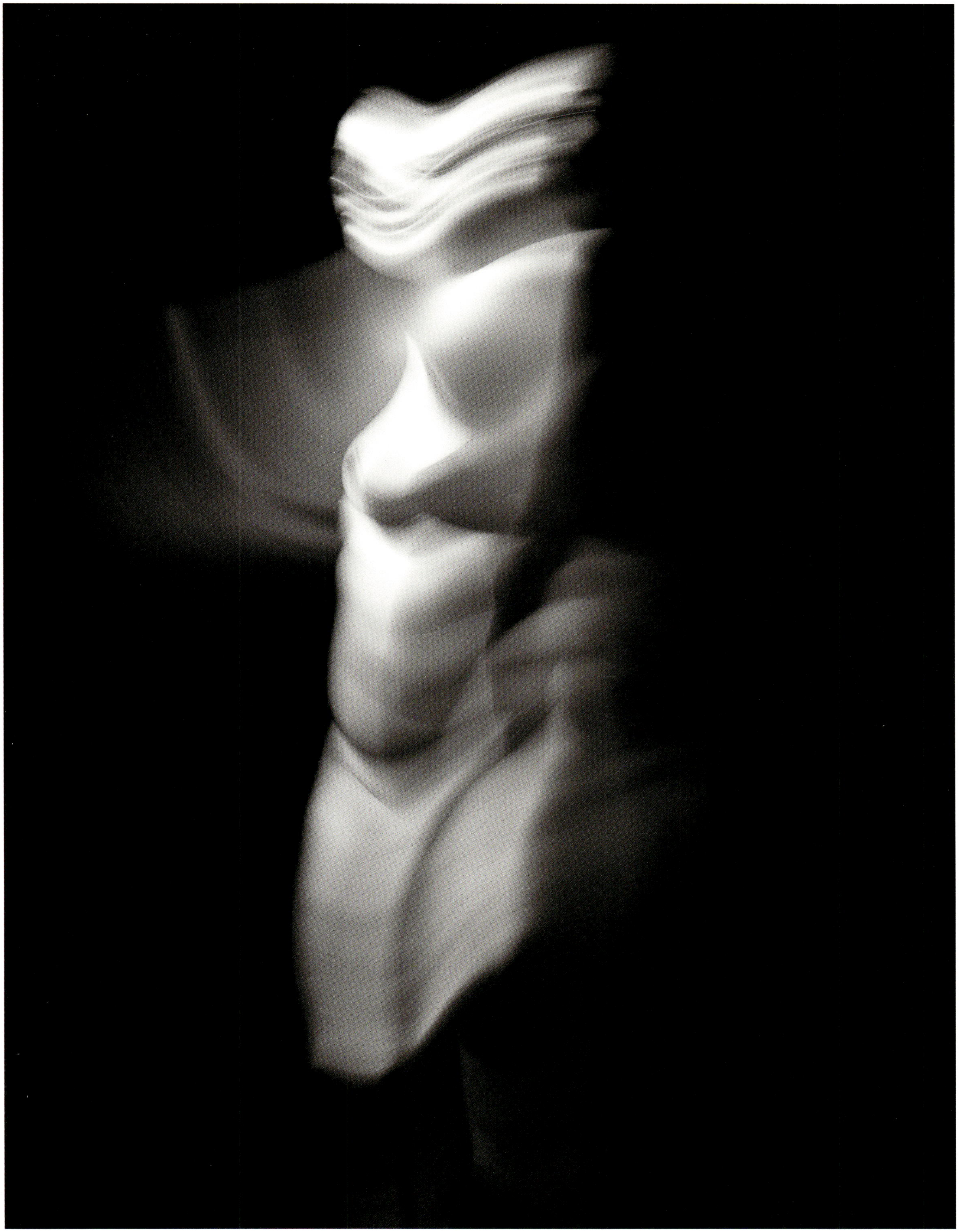

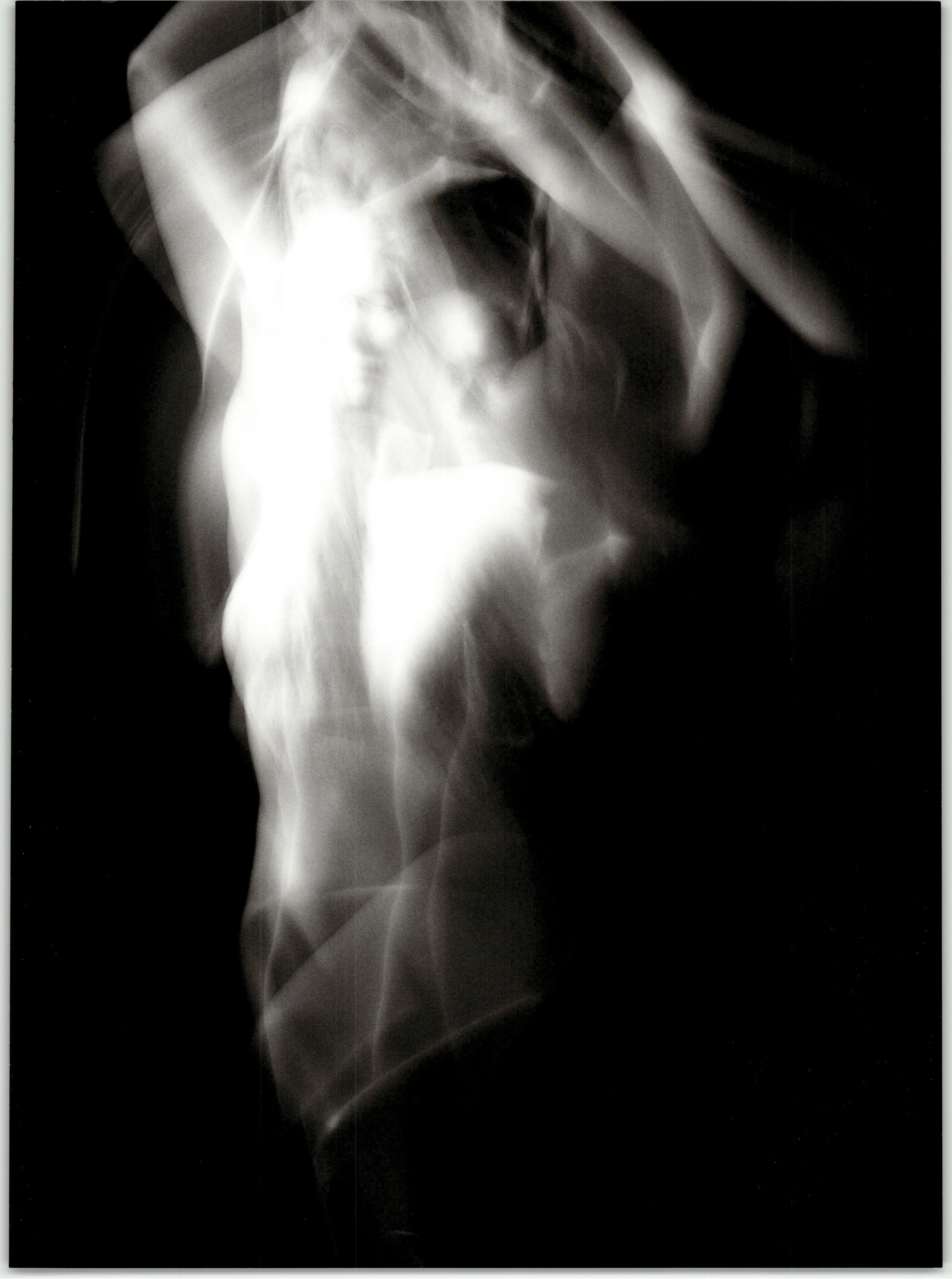

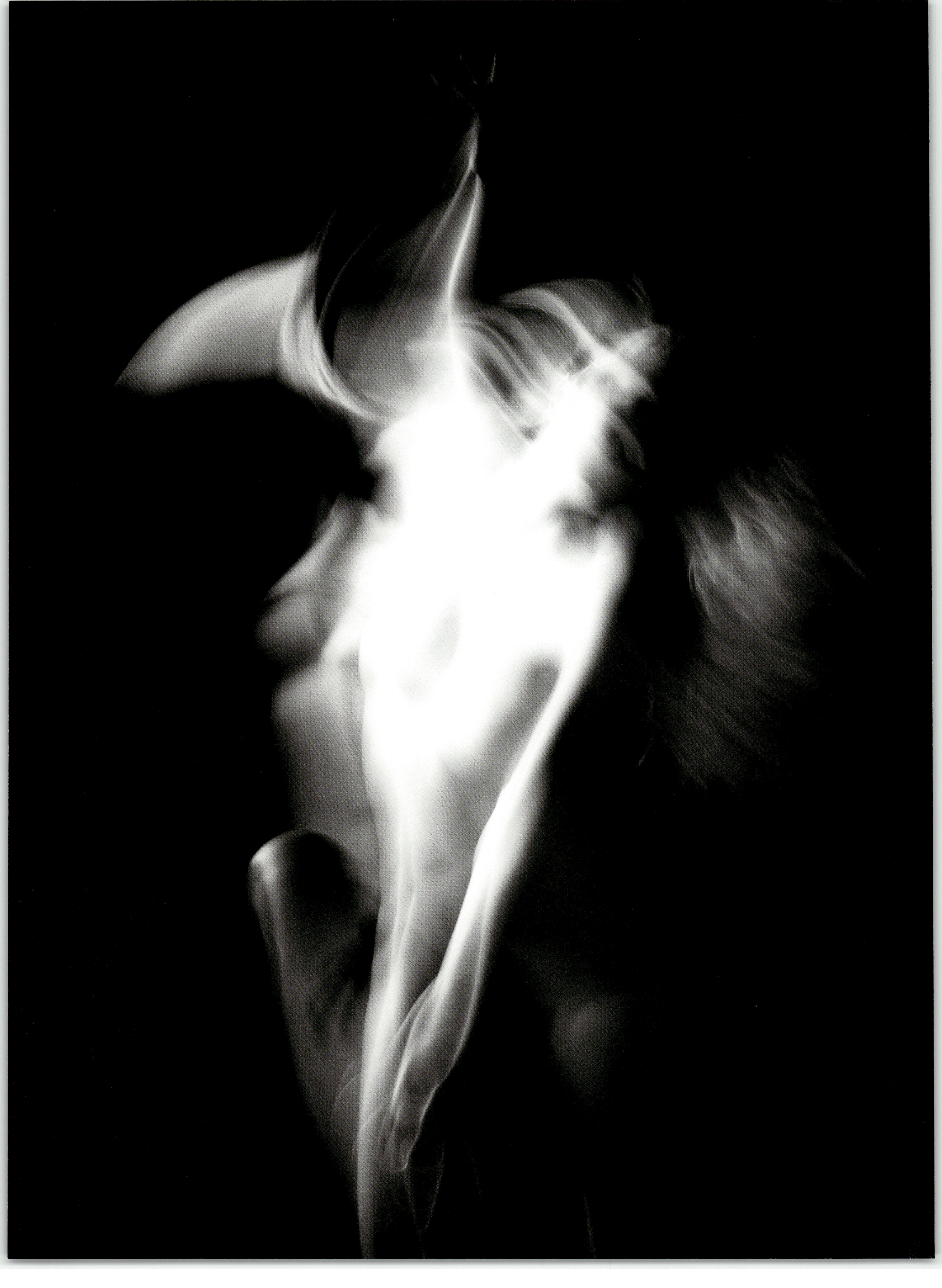

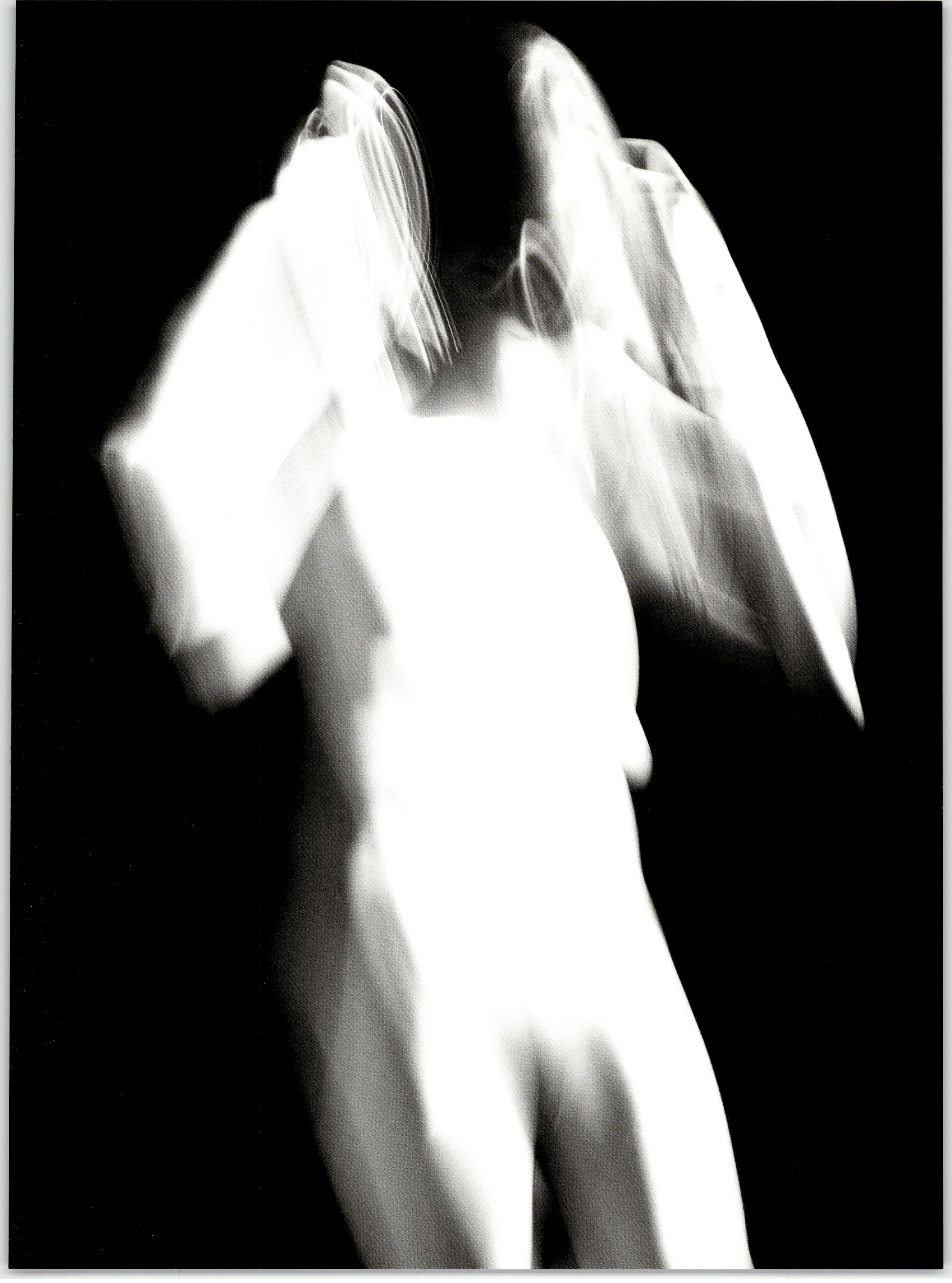

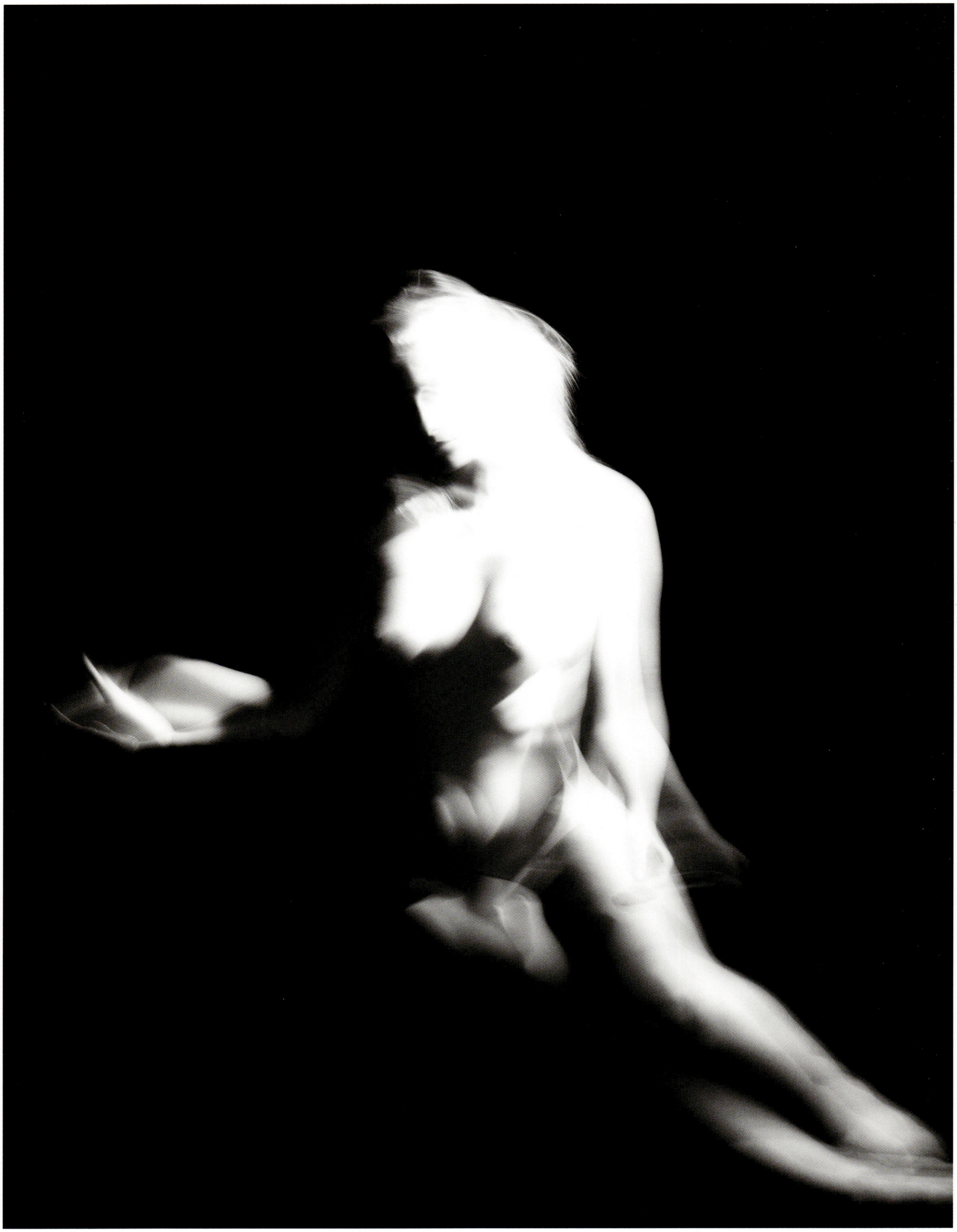

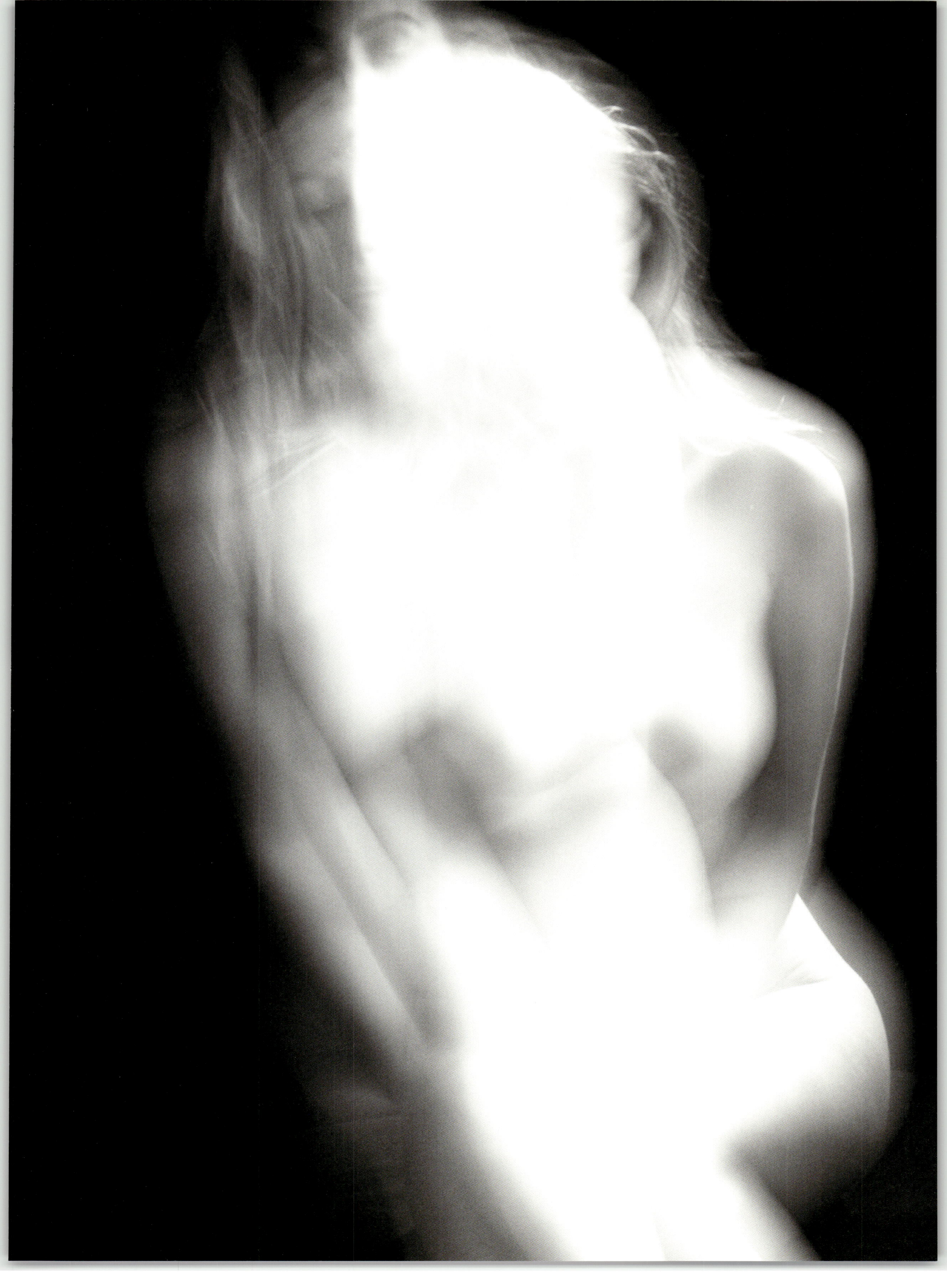

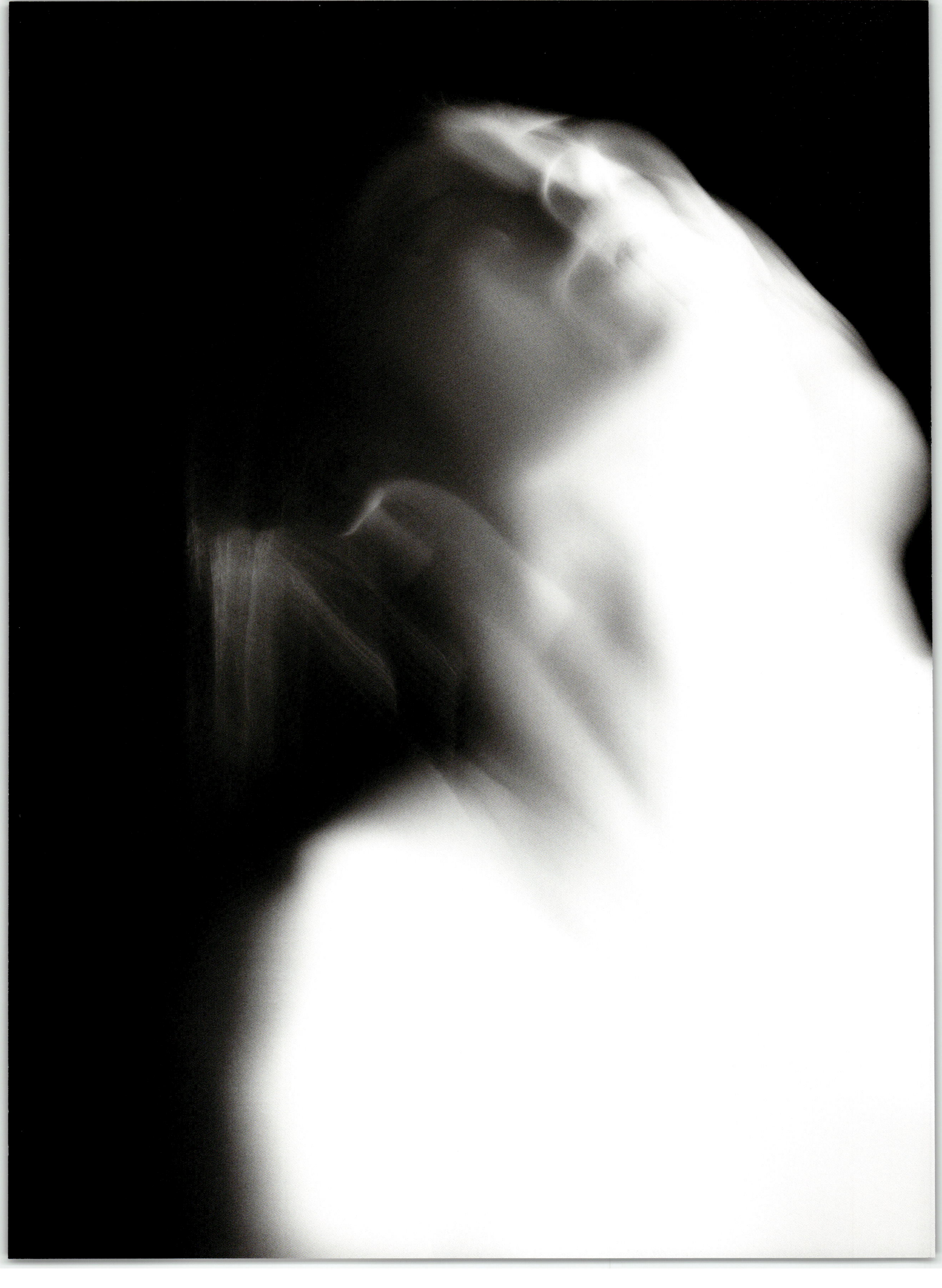

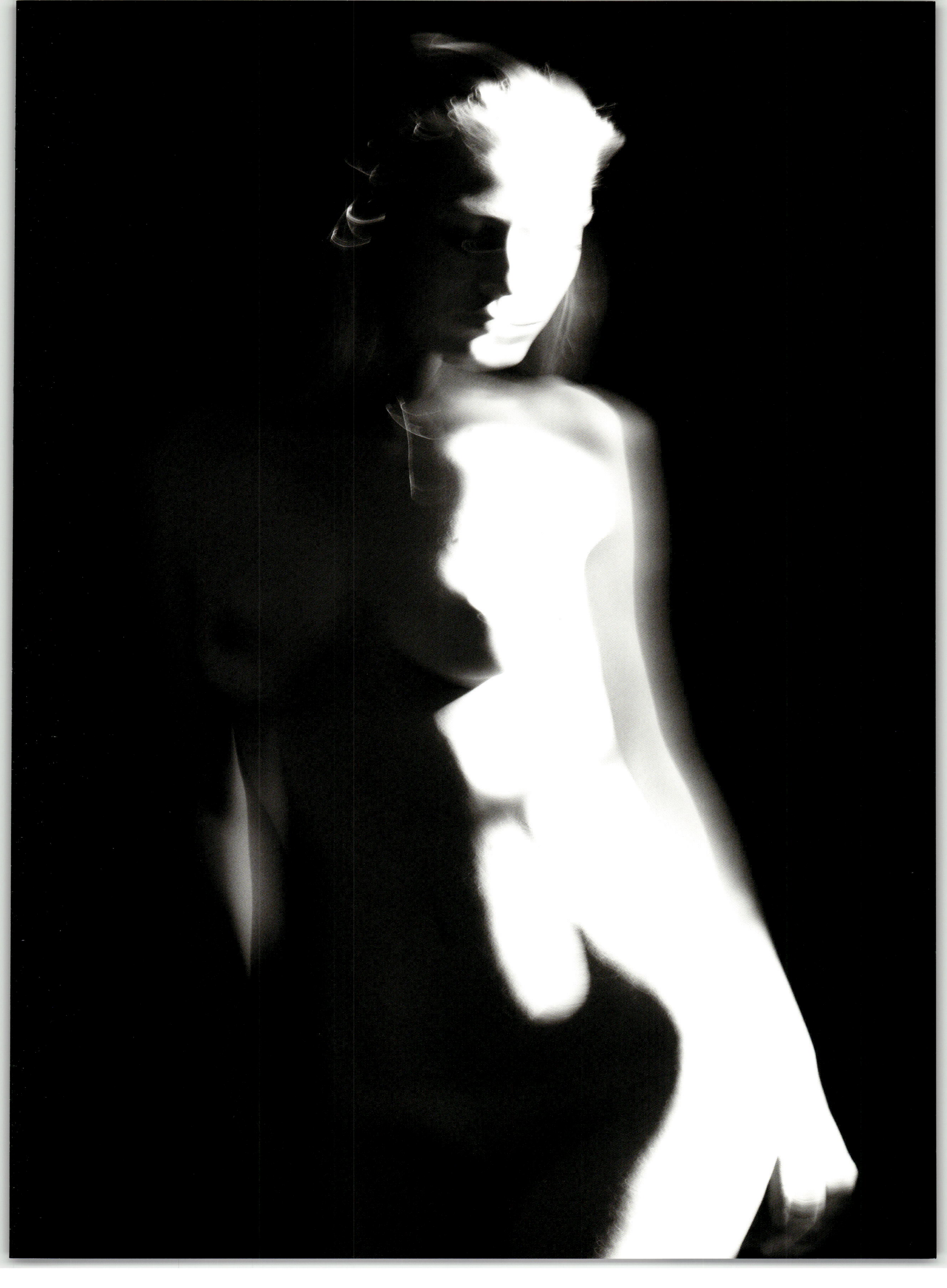

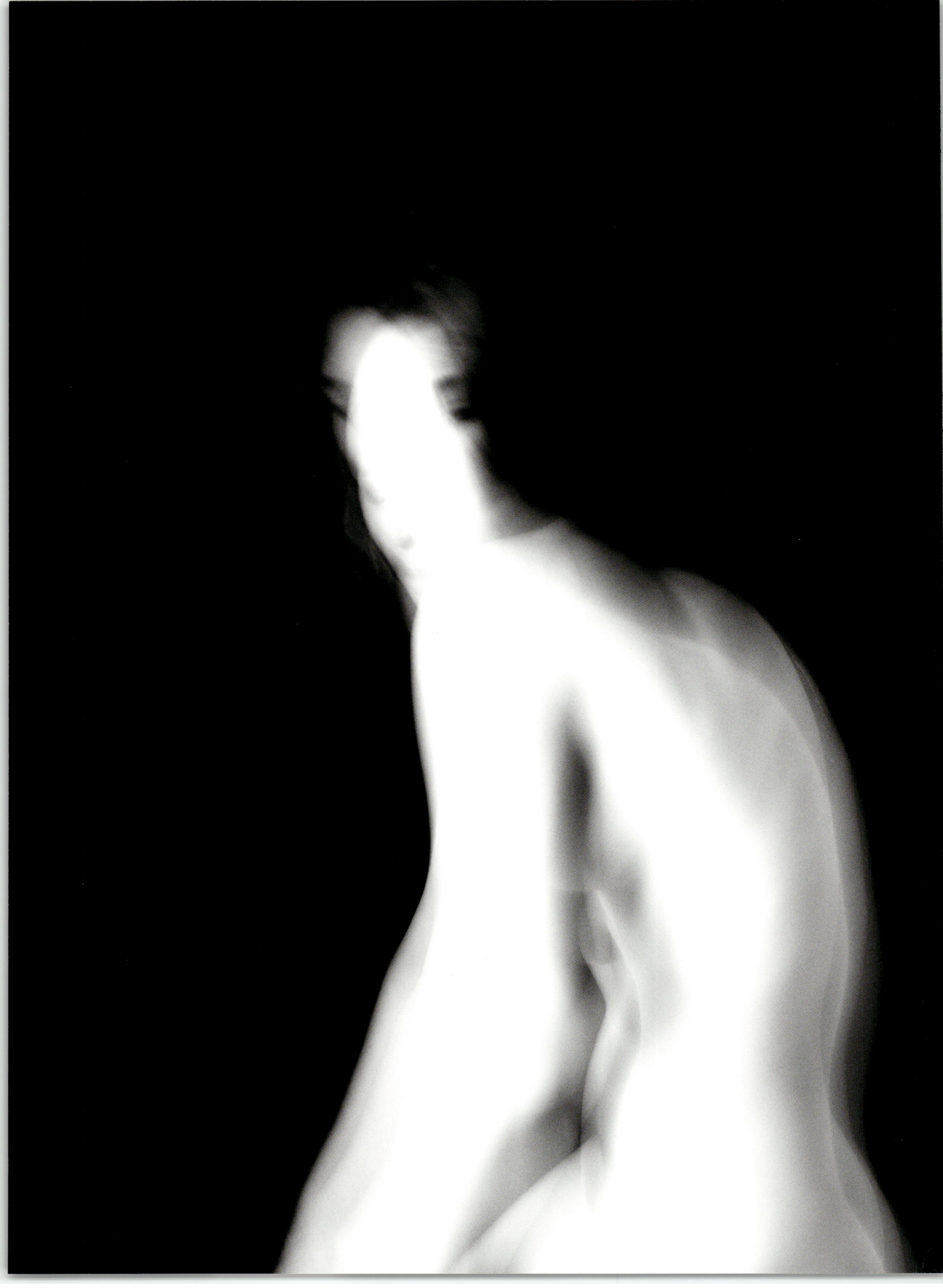

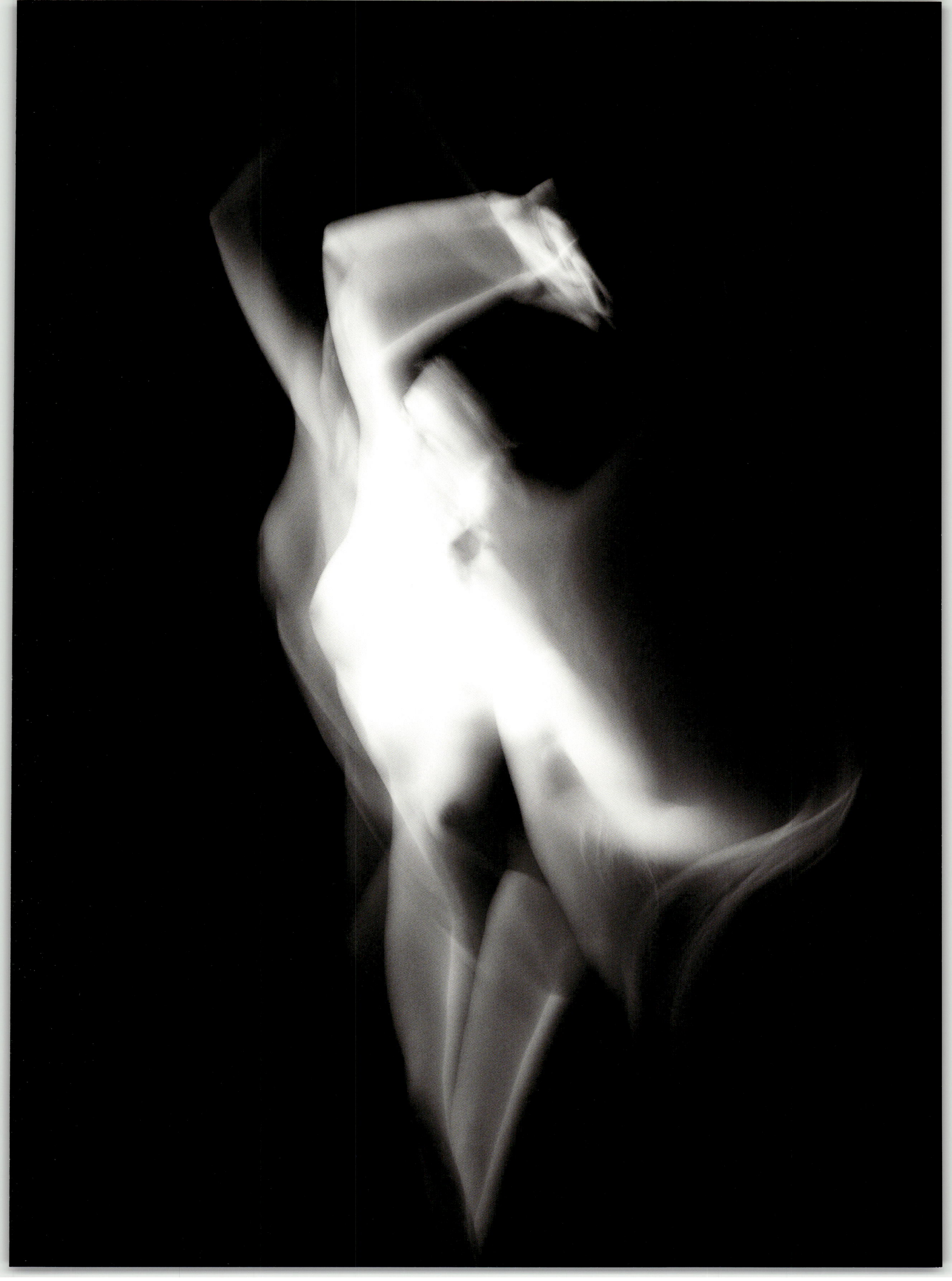

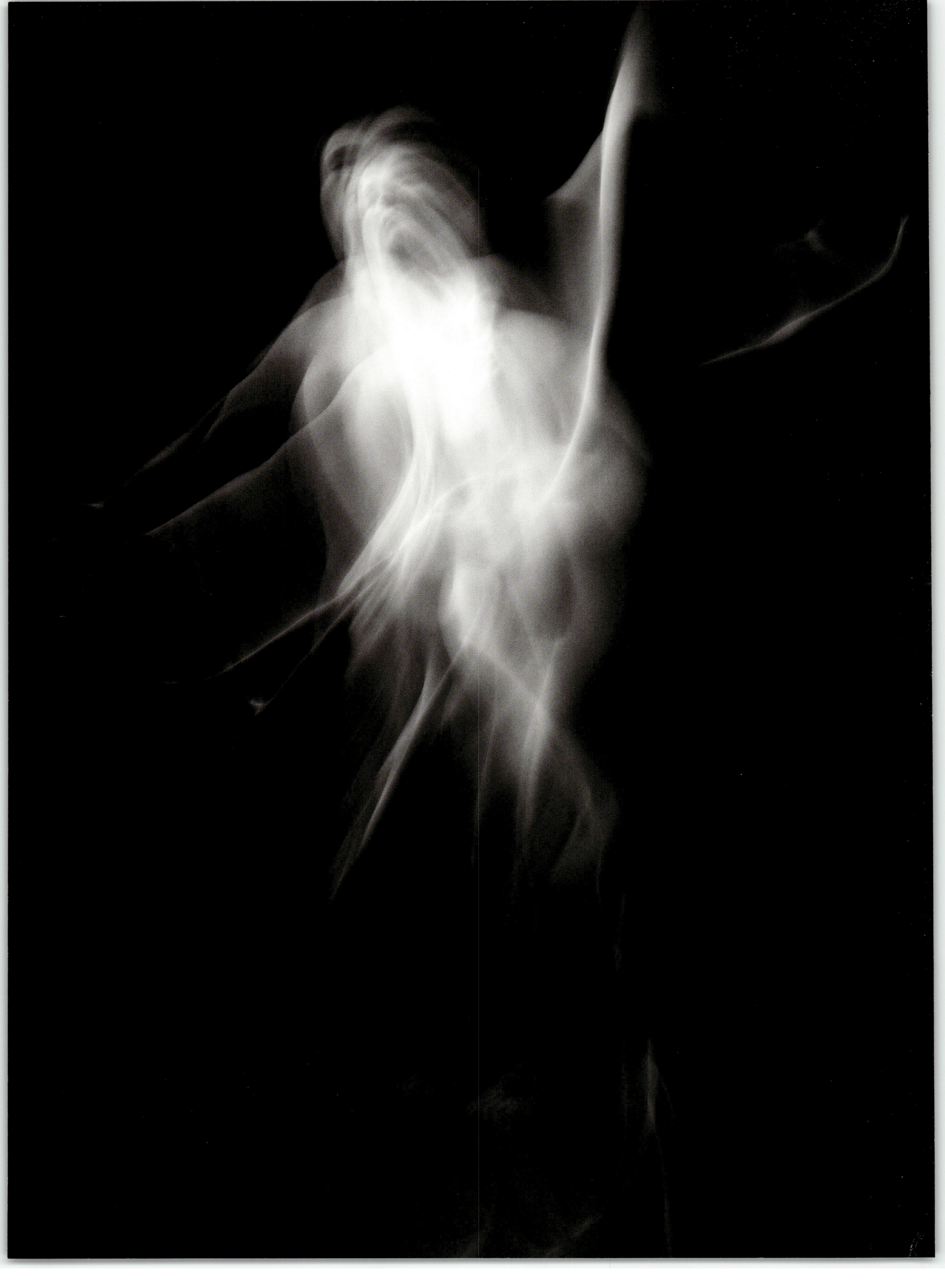

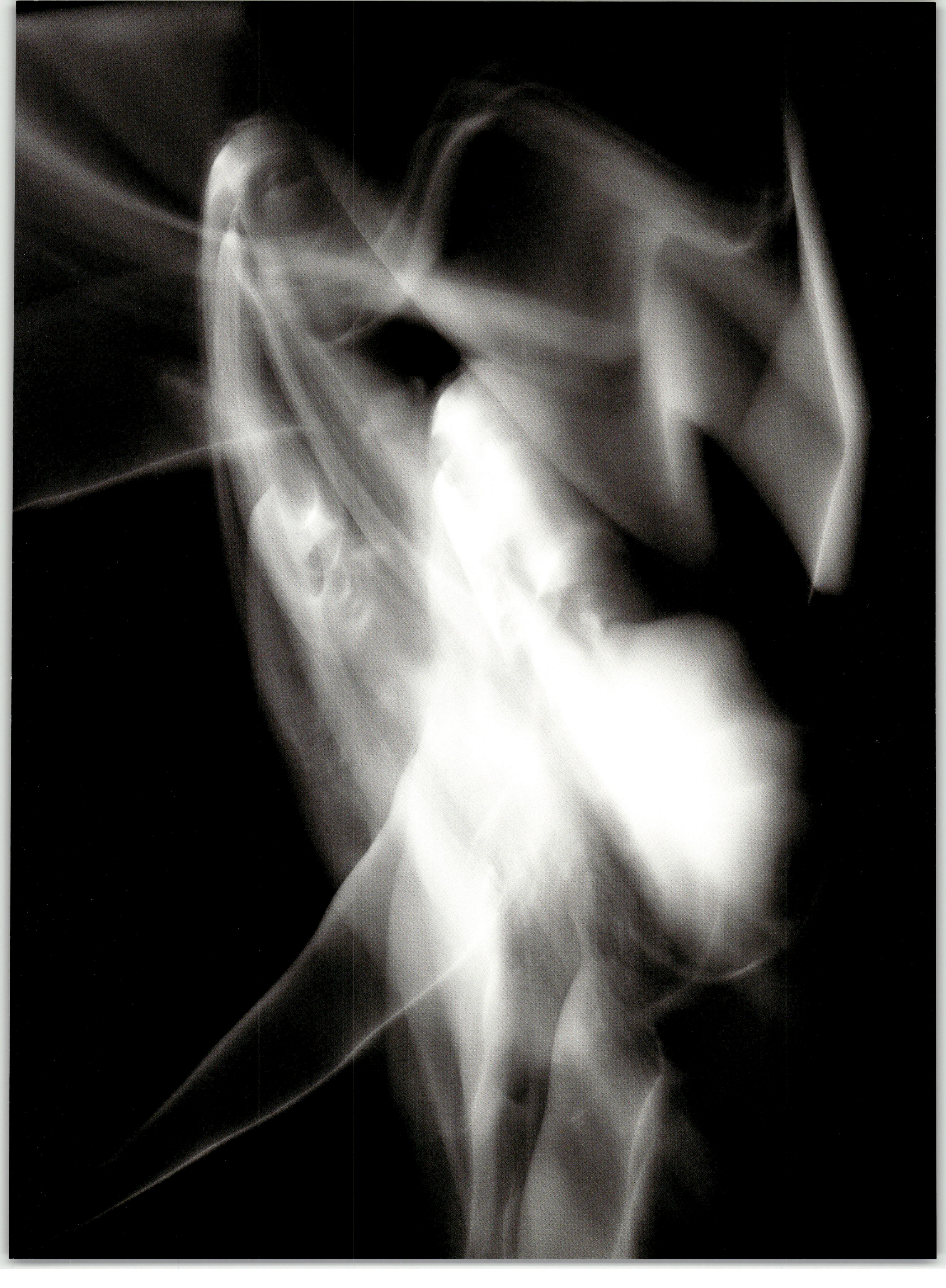

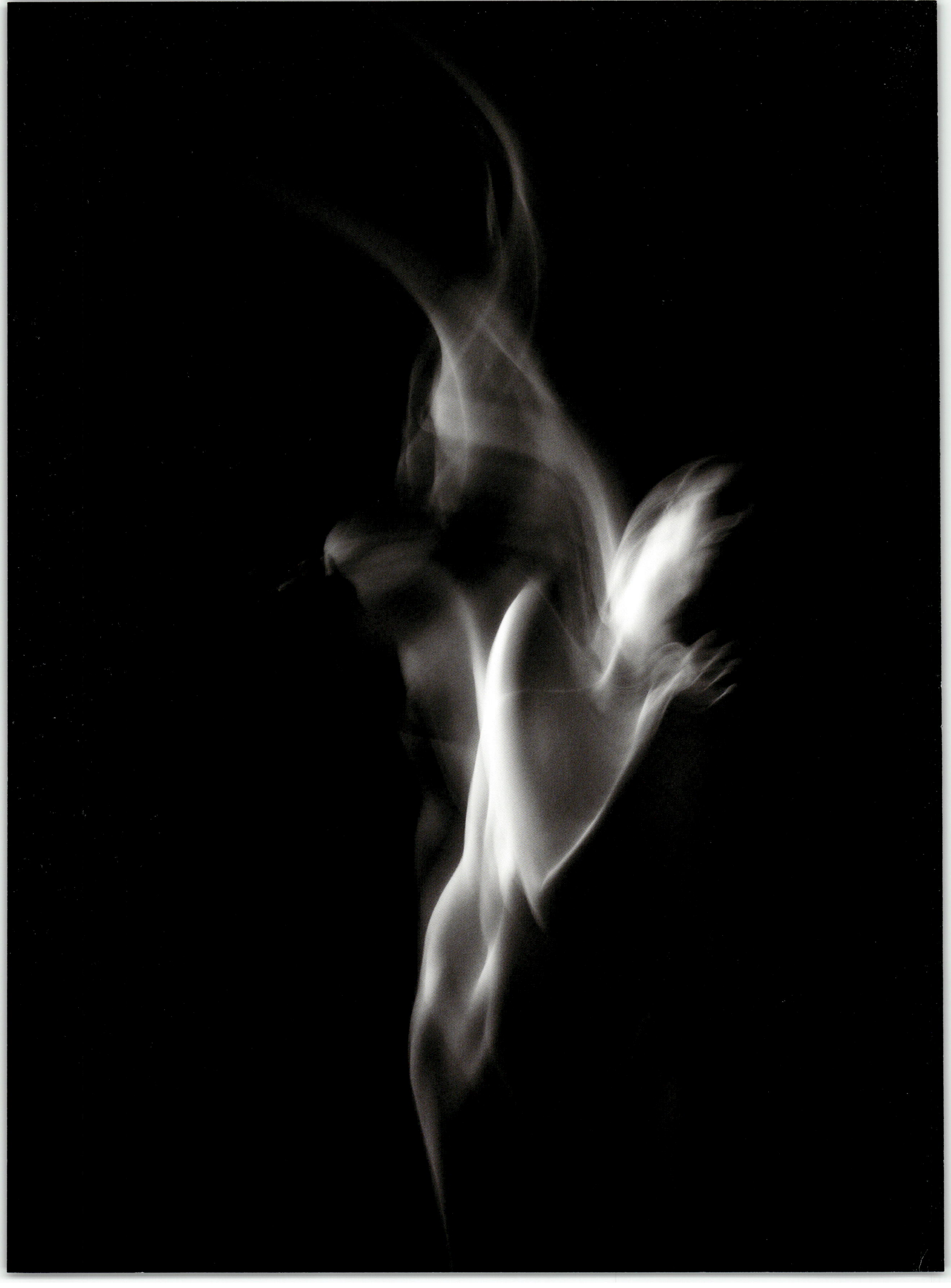

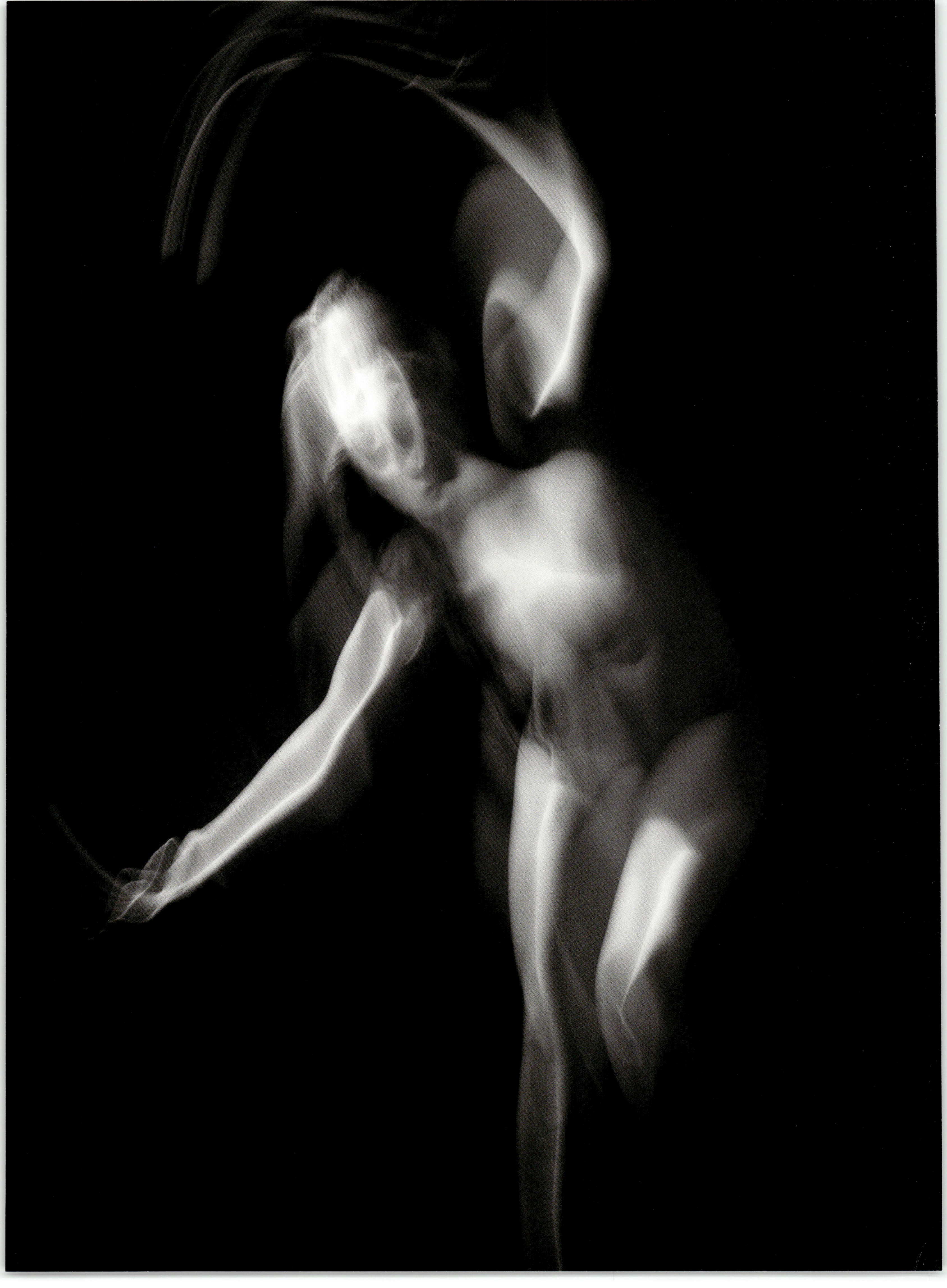

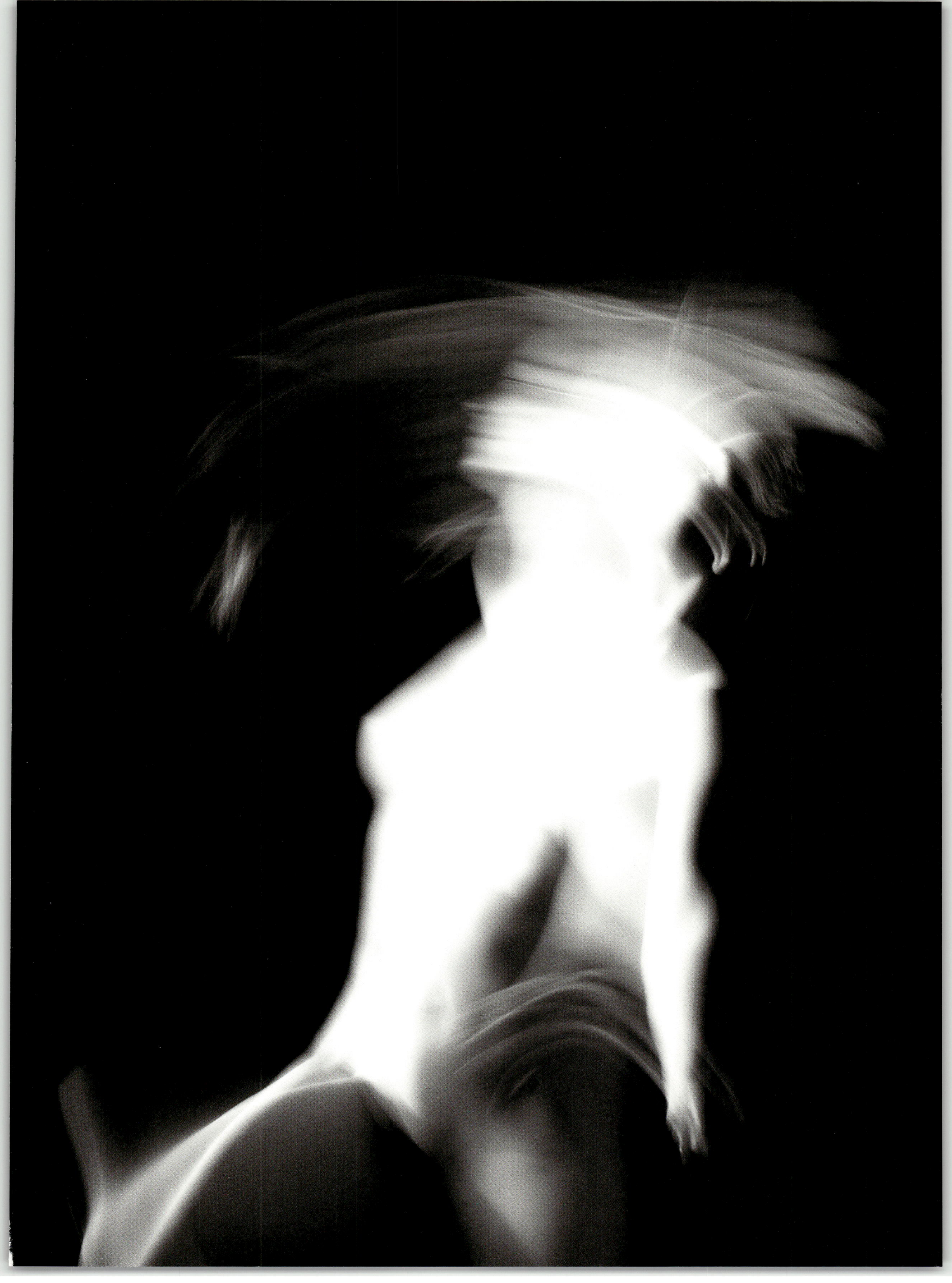

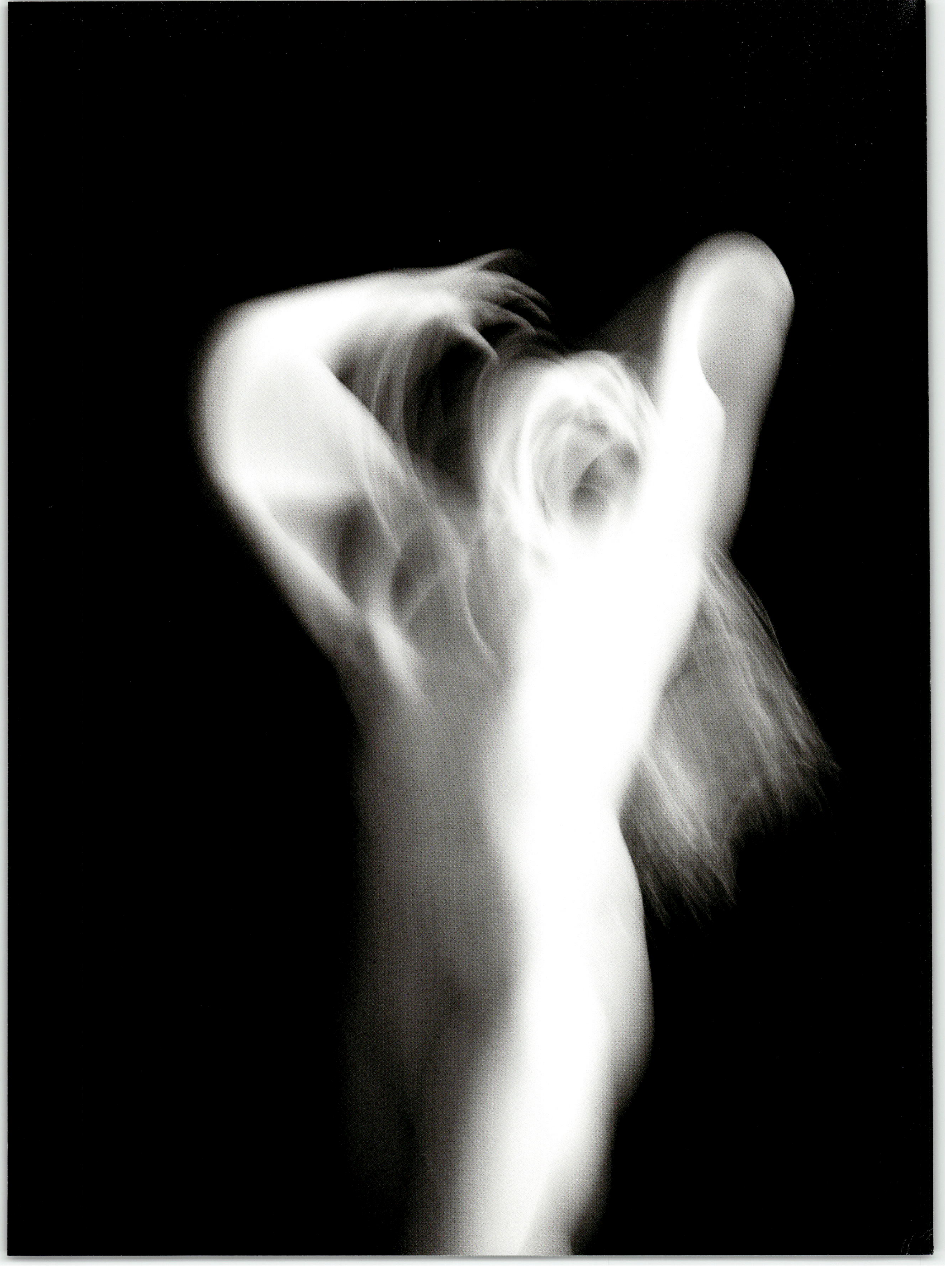

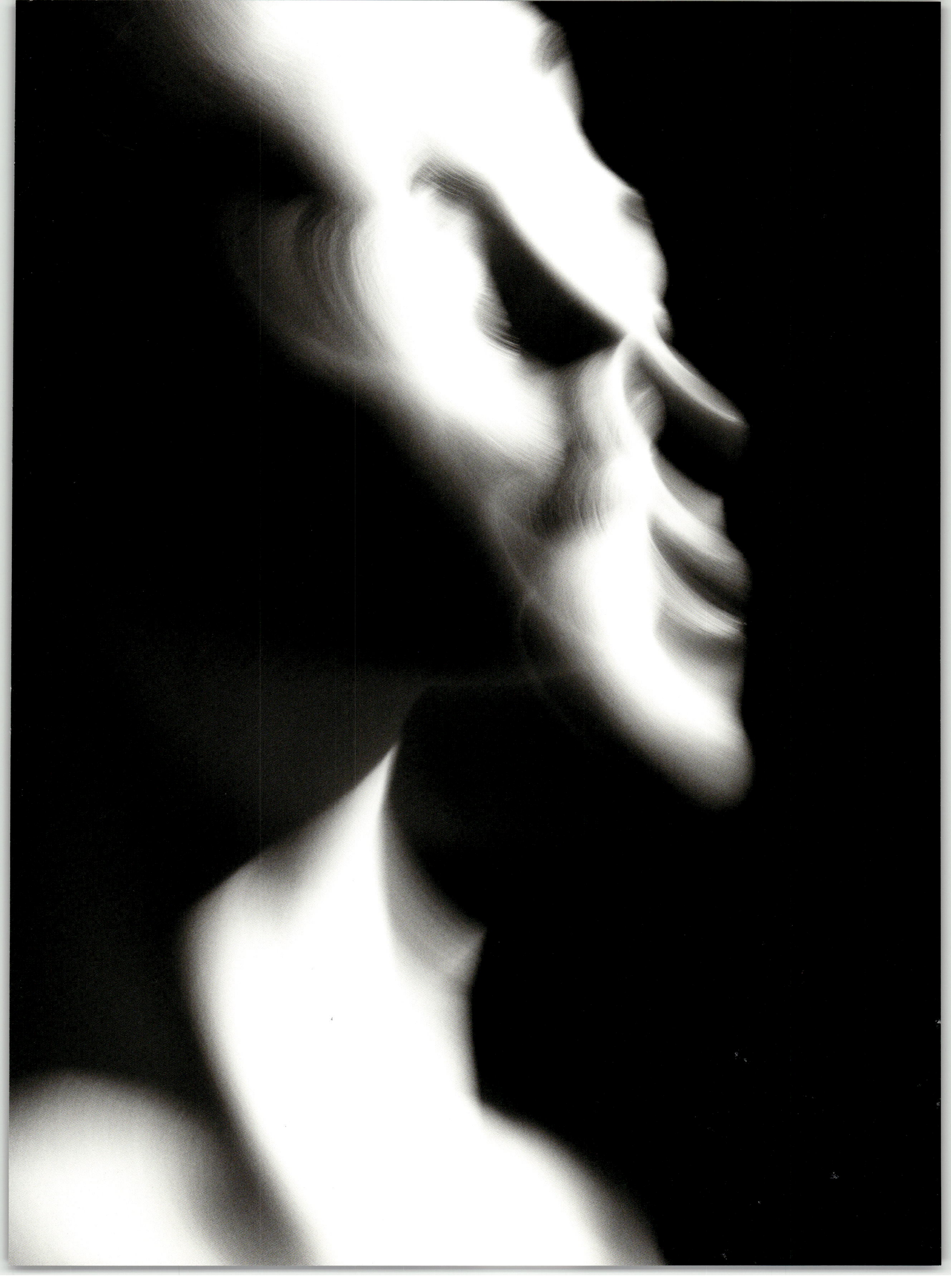

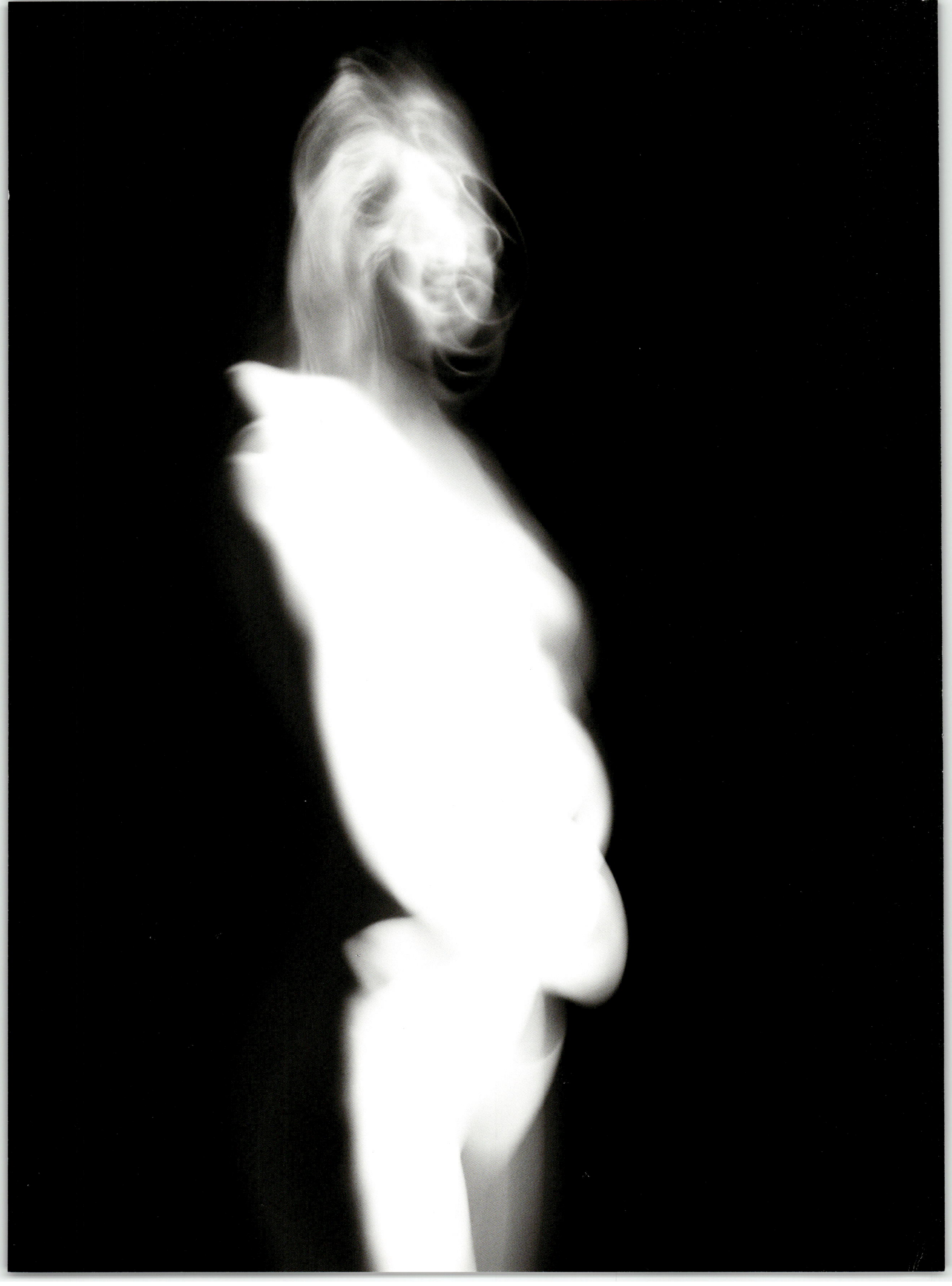

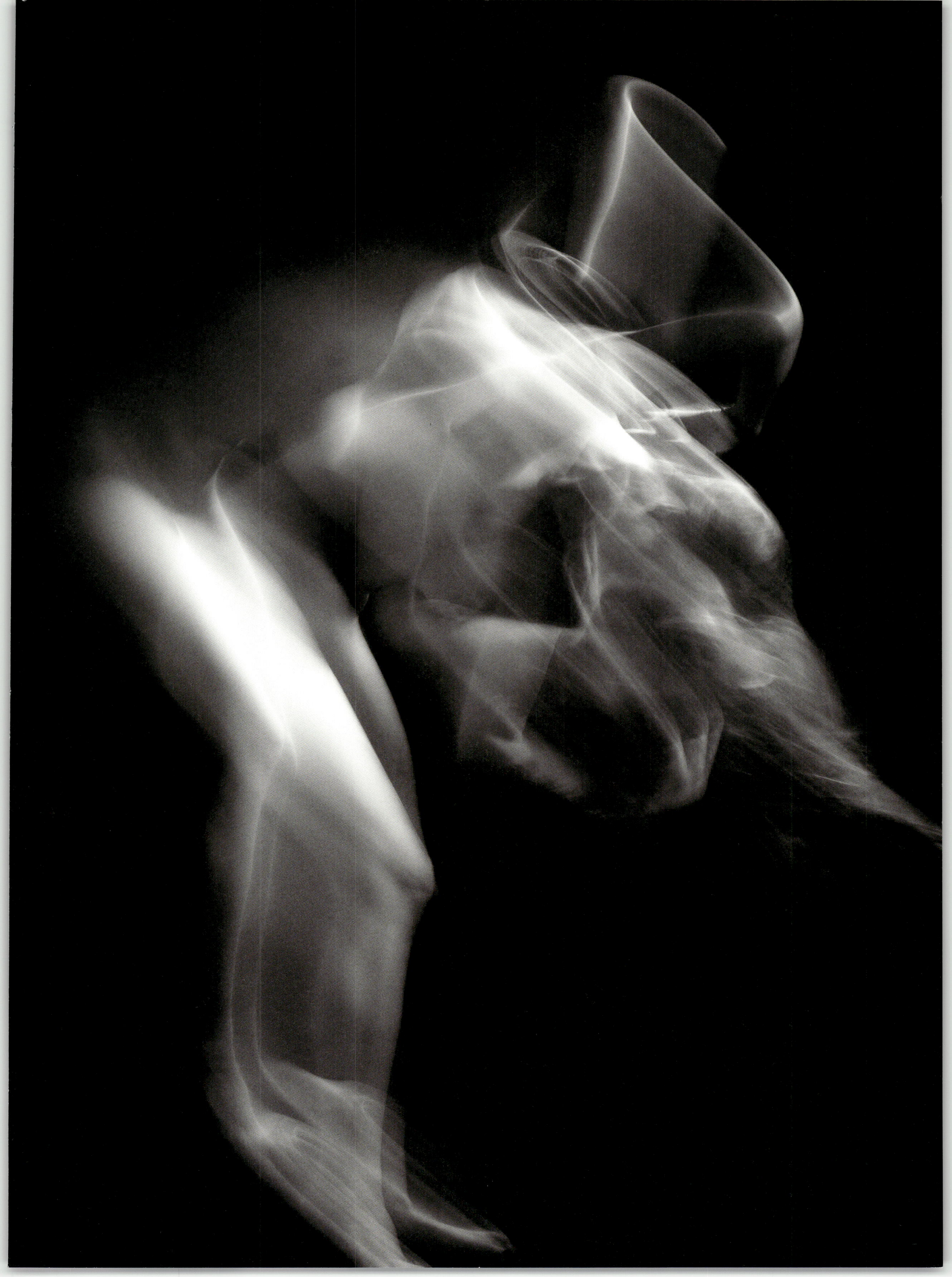

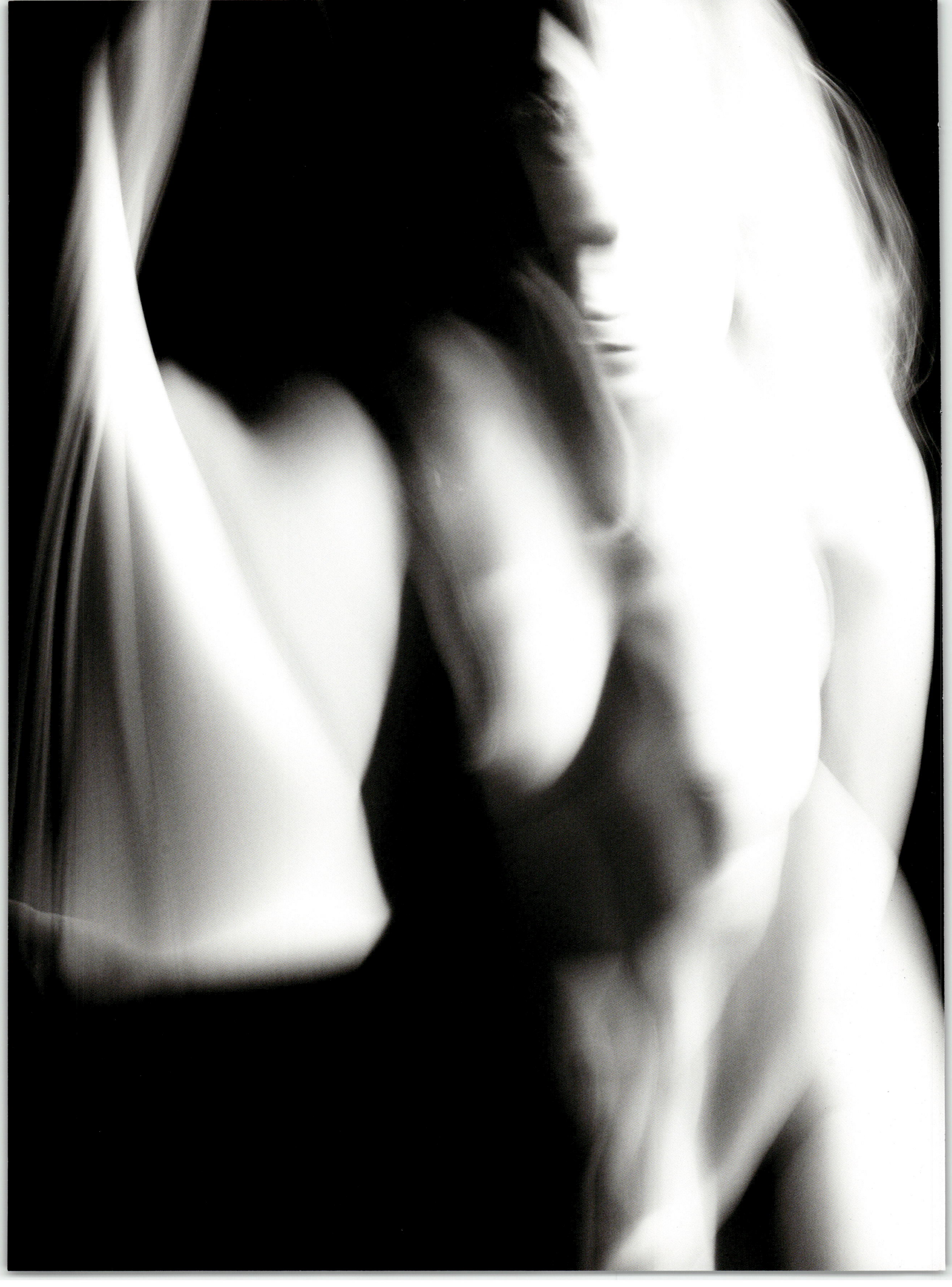

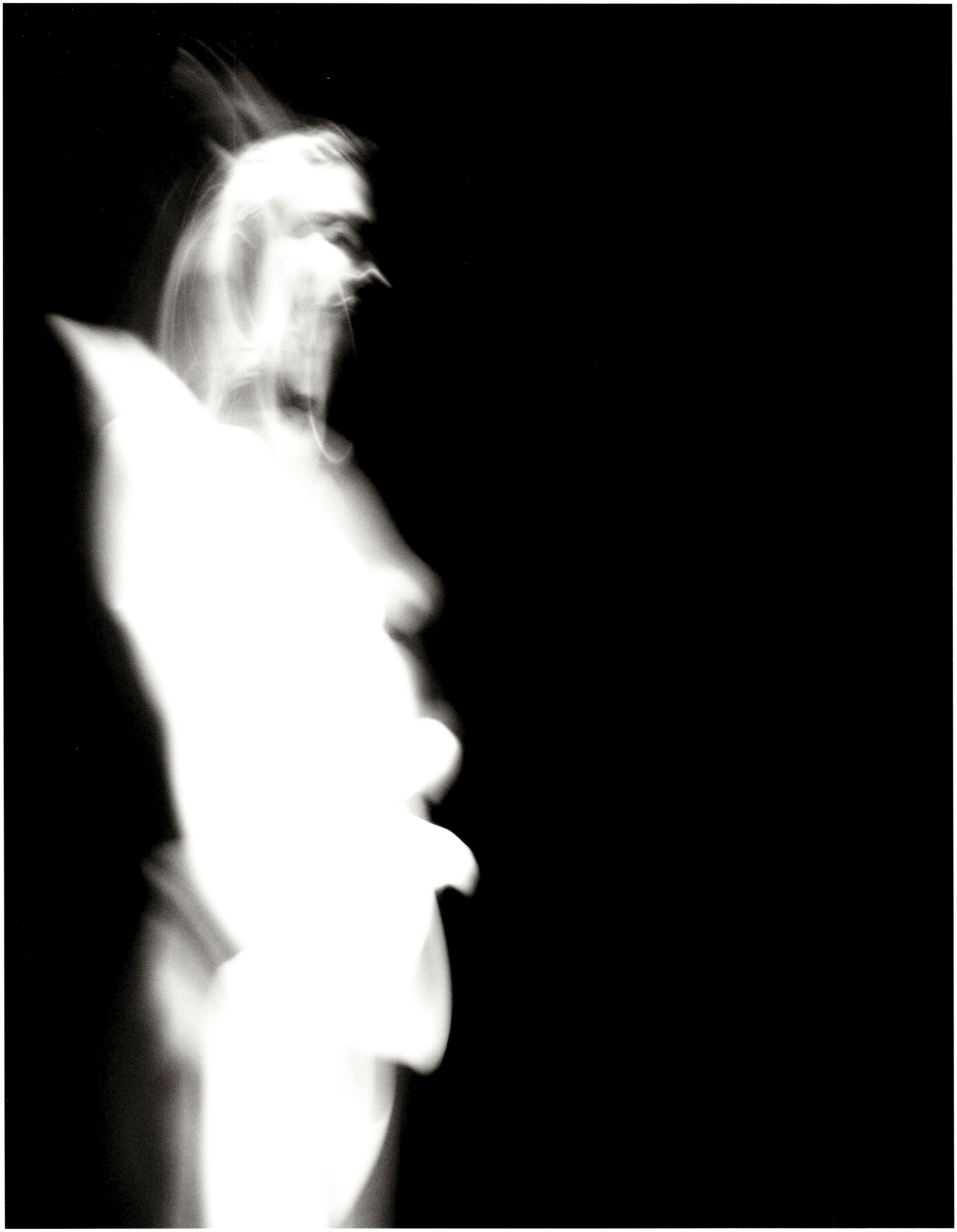

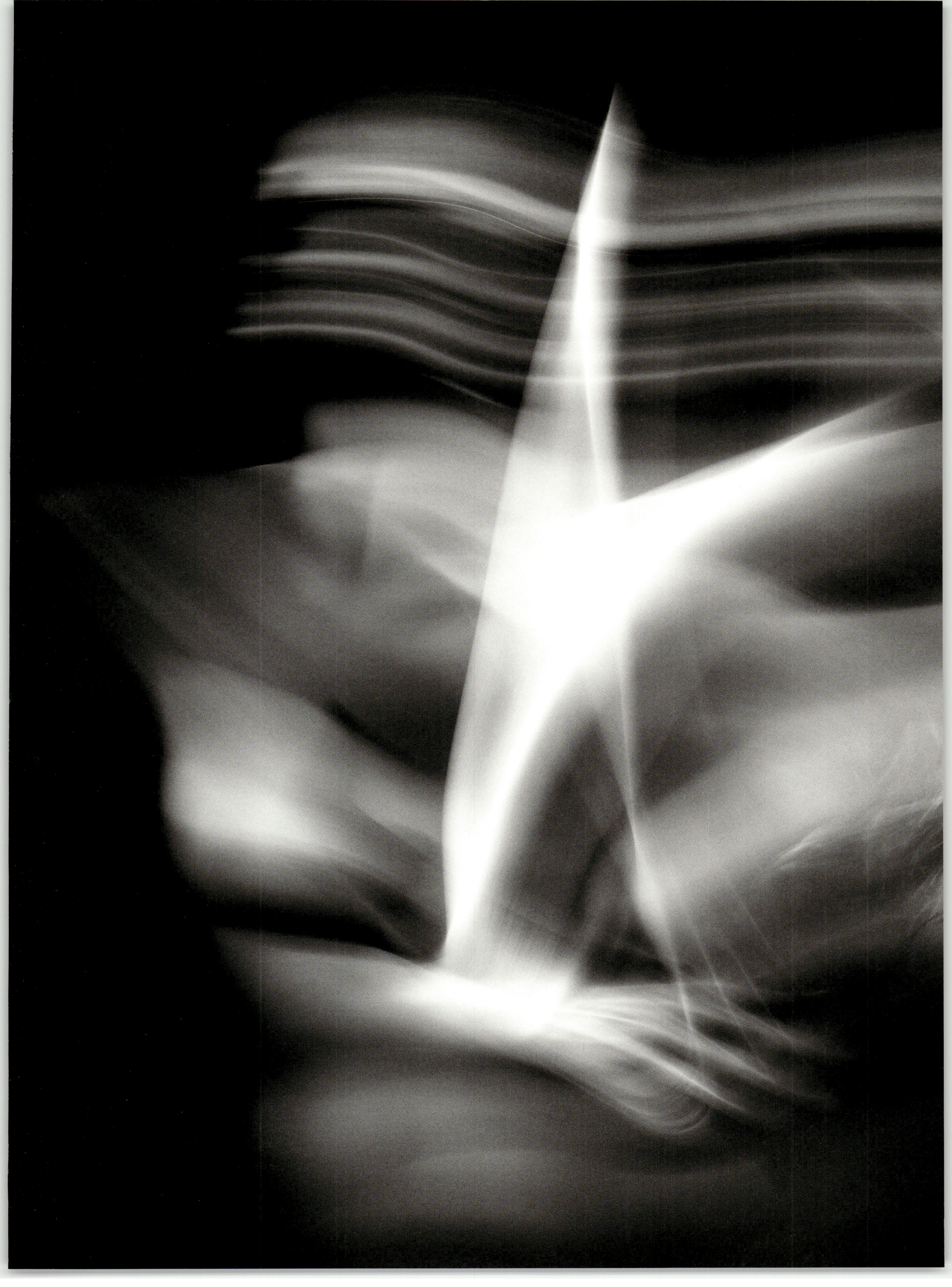

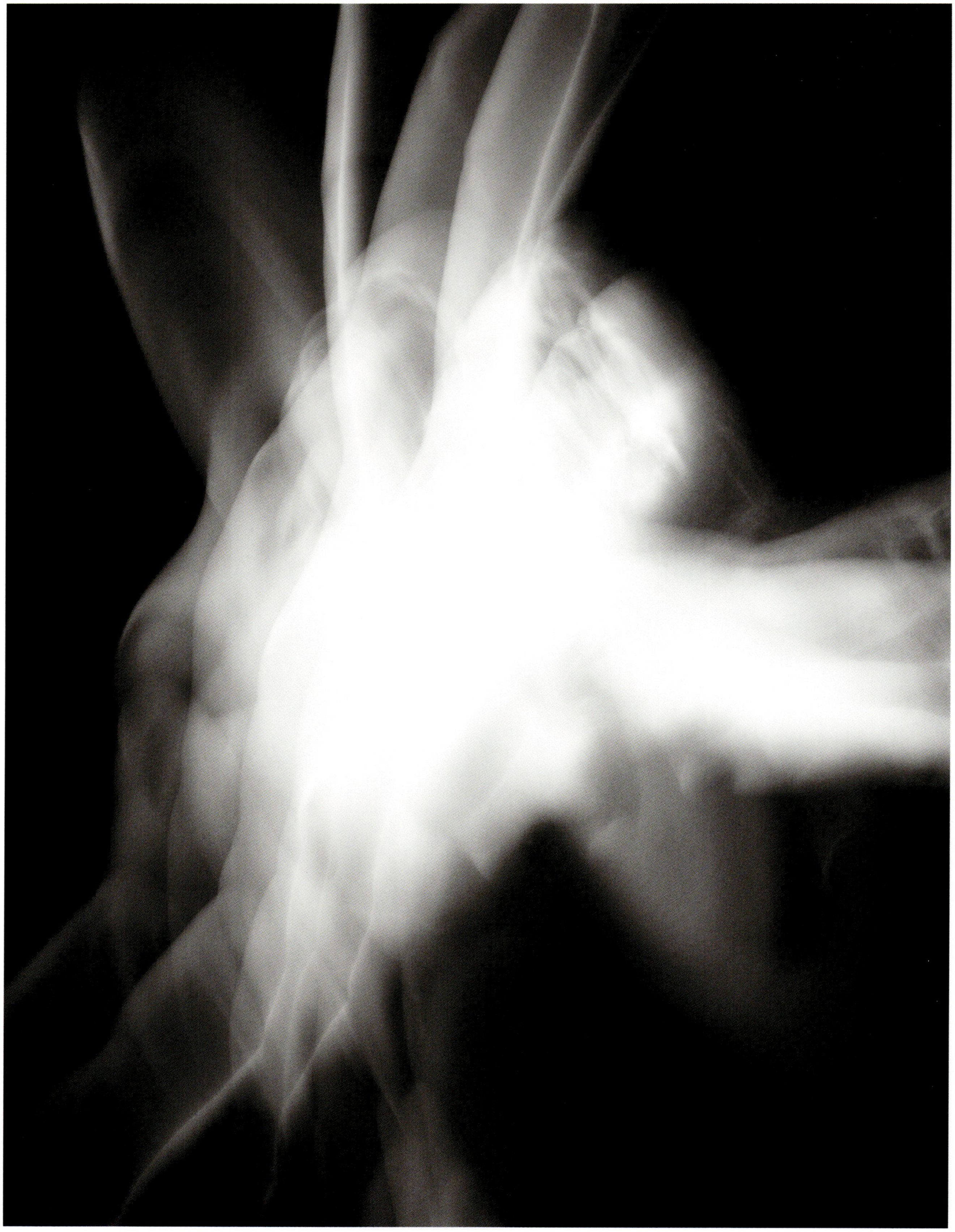

For over two decades Steen Evald has been official photographer for the Danish Royal Family. His fashion images have appeared in various high-profile magazines, such as *Vogue*, *Elle* and *Madame Figaro*, among many others. Evald's evocative images have been exhibited for seven consecutive years at the prestigious juried exhibition "Festival International de la Photographie de Mode" in Cannes. He has worked with a wide spectrum of projects, in recent years focusing on art exhibitions in Denmark and Norway.

Evald lives and works in Copenhagen.

Thanks to Natalya, Rose, Unique Models, Scoop Models, Le Management, Daydream Studio, Julie Ralphs, Claus Due, Eva Frese, Lars Hartmann, Kristoffer Juul, Hanne Klintøe, Magnus Mols, Hanne Muusmann, Hans Jørn Muusmann, Alexander Nyrop, Simon Baungaard, Andreas Pless, Sebastian Vistisen Toft, Caroline Evald Bundgaard and Gustav Evald Bundgaard

And special thanks to Camilla Halvorsen, Nanna Lyhne and Lars Schwander

978 178884 159 7

Edited © Steen Evald & Lars Schwander
Photographs © Steen Evald
Essay © Lars Schwander
Translated by Hanne Klintøe
Designed by Lars Schwander

British Library Cataloguing-in-Publication Data
A catalogue record for this book is available from the British Library

FSC www.fsc.org MIX From responsible sources FSC® C014767

Printed in Belgium
for ACC Art Books Ltd., Woodbridge, Suffolk, England

www.accartbooks.com

ACC ART BOOKS